To Mary Elizabeth

Live in the name of
Christ... as He, in yours —

CHRISTHEART
A WAY OF KNOWING JESUS

Jeanie Miley

Jeanie Miley

SMYTH&HELWYS
PUBLISHING, INCORPORATED · MACON, GEORGIA

SMYTH&
HELWYS

Smyth & Helwys Publishing, Inc.
6316 Peake Road
Macon, Georgia 31210-3960
1-800-747-3016
©1999 by Smyth & Helwys Publishing
All rights reserved.
Printed in the United States of America.

Jeanie Miley

The paper used in this publication meets the minimum
requirements of American National Standard for Information
Sciences—Permanence of Paper for Printed Library Materials.
ANSI Z39.48–1984. (alk. paper)

Library of Congress Cataloging-in-Publication Data

Miley, Jeanie
    ChristHeart: a way of knowing Jesus
    pp.   cm.
    1. Jesus Christ—Biography   Meditations.
    2. Bible.   N.T.   Gospels   Meditations.
    3. Devotional calendars.
    I. Title.
    II. Title: ChristHeart.
    BT306.4.M54   1999
    242'.2—DC21   99-28462
                                                    CIP
ISBN 1-573132-285-8

CONTENTS

KNOW MY POWER

KNOW MY COMPASSION

With deepest gratitude to my fellow-pilgrims in the Seekers Class at River Oaks Baptist Church in Houston, Texas, for your willingness to ask, seek, and knock in new ways in order to find the Truth. Thank you for taking the journey into the heart of Christ.

FOREWORD

Let the same mind be in you that was in Christ Jesus. (Phil 2:5)

Those words of Paul sound so good, but how do you do that? I don't know about you, but I need some help to make words like these from Scripture connect with my life. I need some method or vehicle that interfaces the high ideals of Paul with the concrete life I live day to day. This book Jeanie Miley has written just might be one of those vehicles.

Jeanie's method is so down to earth that it reminds me of the game I played long ago: hide-and-seek. I would stand at the telephone pole with my eyes closed. The other children would run off and have until the count of 25 to hide somewhere in the neighborhood. Then I would have to go out and find them.

As a retreat director, one of my joys is to lead retreatants into a similar game with Scripture. What we seek is the deeper meaning in the words of Jesus. For example, before I read the story of Cana and the changing of the water into wine, I will ask everyone to close their eyes and imagine themselves in a place or person in the story. As I read the story, I ask them to sense what it would be like to listen to the story from that vantage point. I encourage them to take note of what particular wisdom they might find there.

One person might become a water jug in the story and experience the shift of changing from water to a rich wine. Another may choose to be Mary and feel the courage it took for her to command the servants to "do whatever he tells you." This method can take us beyond a familiar story into a deeper meaning that can change our lives.

In Jesus' day the Jewish scholars would weave stories around the scriptures to strengthen the meaning of the story. It was like the framing of a picture, which does not change the painting itself but can greatly enhance its beauty. Jeanie Miley has a gift of taking us with her into the Gospel stories. *Christ-Heart* goes even deeper than her previous book, *Becoming Fire*. Here she asks us to look at the Gospel stories through the eyes of Jesus himself.

When I ask people to go into the Scriptures, rarely does anyone find themselves hiding inside the person of Jesus. Why is this? I'm sure there are many answers to this question. The fact is that Saint Paul clearly directs us to put on the mind of Christ Jesus. *ChristHeart* helps us do just that. First, we must let Jeanie Miley lead us until we begin to feel comfortable looking at the story from Jesus' perspective. But with time, we should be able to do this on our own, even without her help. At that point, the book will have achieved the goal for which it was written.

—Fr. Keith Hosey
Co-Director of John XXIII Center

PREFACE

What is meditation, and is it a Christian practice? How do you practice meditation? In our action-oriented society, why would a Christian want to meditate? Why would anyone want to read another book about Jesus? What would make a person presume to write from his point of view?

Meditation is an ancient practice and discipline that transcends religious boundaries. In the Old Testament we have a record of people who walked and talked with God as a natural way of being. Isaac, for example, meditated in the fields. Moses had direct conversations with the Almighty. The Psalmist implores us to meditate on the laws and wonders of God, on the goodness and lovingkindness of the Sovereign One.

Jesus stayed in constant communication with his father, drawing apart from the disciples to go to the lake or the mountaintop to pray, and when he taught us to "abide in him" (John 15), he was asking us to learn to live in unhindered relationship and communication with the Father. Meditation is what we do to facilitate that relationship.

For contemporary Christians who are accustomed to action and a results-oriented style of prayer, meditation may or may not feel natural. *ChristHeart* provides a gentle method of receptive, open-hearted prayer. It introduces a manner of nurturing the habit of practicing the presence of Christ. Using Scripture as its base, *ChristHeart* is a simple method, but it almost guarantees profound changes of the mind and heart.

ChristHeart is unique in that it provides a means of getting acquainted with Christ by mulling over the incidents in his life. It invites us to enter deeply into the experiences of the human Jesus by spending seven days contemplating each event, using our imaginations to see what he saw and to hear what he heard. The meditations in this book encourage us to put ourselves in the shoes of Jesus and become aware of his thoughts, feel his heartbeat, and identify with his desires.

The "how" of knowing Christ is incredibly simple. *Christ-Heart* invites us to go on a profound journey of discovery that begins by reading a passage in the Gospels every day for a week. At times a parallel or complementary passage may be suggested. It is helpful to read that passage at least three times. Then, read one of the devotionals that invites you to use your imagination and to picture yourself in that scene as Jesus might have been in it. Use *ChristHeart* as a devotional guide to carry with you as you go about the demands of your daily activities. Use it to enhance a daily quiet time, or on an extended personal retreat, or as a discussion starter for a small group experience.

To glean the most from each day's meditation, have a set time and place each day for reading and praying. Choose a theme from Jesus' life or follow the events of his life in chronological order. While it is suggested that you use one reading each day, you may want to go at a faster or slower pace. Just as the Living Christ meets each one at the point of individual need, *ChristHeart* can be adapted to suit your need and style.

Begin by taking a few minutes to quiet your mind and collect your thoughts, breathing deeply and reminding yourself that you are, wherever you are, already in the presence of Christ. Ask him to guide your mind to the truth he wants for you.

Read the Scripture for the day and then just "sit with it" for a few moments, waiting to see what insights might come to you. Read the meditation from *ChristHeart* slowly, savoring each impression. See the scenes and the people in the event. Hear the sounds. Taste, smell, and feel what is in the story. Allow all of your senses to be involved. Ask the Holy Spirit to work at his pace and give him the time he needs to reveal the truth he wants for you.

If you desire, use a journal to record your impressions. Perhaps you might write your prayers to God. If you sense that God is speaking to you through the story or through an impression, record what you think God might be saying. As you stay with this method, you will come to discern when the impression is from God and when it is not. If nothing happens, don't give up. Instead, accept whatever happens in the experiences as exactly what God intends to happen for that day. Sit quietly with an open mind and a willing heart for at least twenty minutes.

Use each day's meditation as a seed for contemplation, turning it over and over in your mind, or take the passage with you and in moments throughout your day call that scene to mind and see if the Living Christ wants to reveal something to you. Often God will break into your awareness with a surprising insight. When this happens, record the sacred moment in your journal.

A question or two at the end of each meditation will help you connect the passage with your personal life. You may want to write about this question, or perhaps you could use it as the beginning of a dialogue with the Living Christ. If you are involved in a relationship with a spiritual director or in a spiritual growth group, use the questions and insights as prompters for dialogue in these relationships.

The purpose of *ChristHeart* is to facilitate your personal, vital love-relationship with Christ, to provide a means for you to know him in a powerful, present-tense way, and to give you a sense of his heart. As you grow in empathy with Jesus, you will discover more about your own humanity. As you enter into his experiences, you will find new meaning for your own life experiences. As you come to know Christ better, you will experience the empowerment of the Holy One. As you spend more time identifying with the thoughts, feelings, and actions of the human/divine Jesus, you will come to a clearer understanding of who you are and who you are intended to be.

The Living Christ will honor your efforts and your journey. He will, if you commit the process to him, lead you where you need to go. If you will give up your preconceived notions of how you think your spiritual growth should happen, Christ's Spirit will do exactly what needs to be done in your mind, heart, and will. As you identify more and more with Christ's heart, your own heart will be set free.

As much as possible, simply suit up and show up for your daily meditation. Don't concern yourself with the results. Don't look here and there for proof that it's working. Instead, simply trust that the Living Christ will break into your life to instruct and guide you. Most of all, this means of praying will provide a way for the Risen Lord to love you. In time, Jesus Christ will give you a new heart, and then you will be set free.

---

* In selecting only thirty-four experiences from the life of Jesus, it was necessary to make the painful choices of leaving out certain events and encounters. Once the method of *ChristHeart* is learned, you can then enter into any of the scenes in Jesus' life and glean the truth of it for your own life.

INTRODUCTION

"Never assume that the members of your congregation have a clue about who Jesus is," our seminar speaker told us. "And don't take for granted that the chairpersons of your church committees know Jesus as their personal Savior and Lord."

One of the country's most articulate spokesmen and pastors had spoken the truth. Like the messages of all prophets, his message stung. The room became uncomfortably quiet.

Late one night, only six months earlier, I had driven down the Katy Freeway in Houston, Texas, pondering a lecture I had presented to my class at the Spiritual Direction Institute of the Cenacle Retreat House. We had spent the evening studying Christology, the study of Christ. When I arrived home, the first thing I said to my husband (before "How was your day?") was: "The problem with churches is that there is no Christology any more. People don't know what it means to believe in Christ or to have a personal relationship with him."

My pastor-husband surely must have thought it was too late at night to discuss such heavy topics, but, to his credit, he put down his cereal bowl and listened intently. Since that night, each of us has seen the truth of our discovery more and more. Since that night, too, we have made it a goal to have some teaching about Jesus, the Son of God, going on in our church at all times.

Perhaps the American church has lost its power because it has lost its Person. Perhaps it has been so molded by the culture that it has slipped from its foundation. Perhaps we have gotten so involved in peripheral concerns because we have forgotten our primary concern. Perhaps contemporary Christians need to discover the person of the historical Jesus and the power and presence of the Living Christ if they are to live the abundant life Jesus promised.

"We're going to study the life and teachings of Jesus Christ," I announced to the Singles Sunday School Class of my church. "Beginning next Sunday." I walked out of that Sunday School class thinking to myself, *What in the world are you doing? You can't teach the life and work of Christ. You haven't even been to seminary.* All through the worship service I sat in stunned disbelief at the spontaneous decision I had made, but I had committed myself. In front of a whole room of witnesses I had made my declaration, and so I began to gather my research materials.

Martus, my husband, brought home his syllabus and lecture notes from his seminary class files and his days of teaching at the college level. I searched the bookstore for the latest books on Jesus. I rediscovered my *Harmony of the Gospels*.

Every time I sat down to study, I was filled with self-doubt. I tried to think of a way out, an easier path. Why didn't I just teach from the curriculum that had been prepared by professionals, as I had done for years? Did the members of my class, I wondered in my weakest moments, really want to know about Jesus? Yet, every time I began to research and study the material, I became filled with energy and excitement. It was as if merely reading about the life of the Carpenter from Nazareth gave me courage and boldness I didn't know I had. As I surrendered to the study of the facts, the Living Christ, through the power of the Holy Spirit, literally fired my imagination with creativity and warmed my heart with a love that would not let me go. Week by week the Living Christ put a light in my path so that I could see where I was going . . . and where I was taking my students.

Since that life-changing Sunday nearly fifteen years ago, I have taught the life of Christ from various aspects. In addition to teaching Jesus' life chronologically, sometimes I teach only one of the Gospels at a time. I have spent a whole year exploring the Sermon on the Mount in Matthew 5 and 6 and the parables and miracles. I have even developed an entire retreat experience around the four prayer requests Jesus made in John 17 and another on the Lord's Prayer!

However I approach the story, I never cease to be captured anew by the power of his presence. Moreover, since introducing people to a personal, vital love-relationship with the Living Christ has become my passion, I have experienced grace and peace in the midst of some of the most difficult years of my life. Indeed, as I continue leading, I teach what I want to learn more than anything else.

ChristHeart takes a bold step—and an audacious one at that—in an attempt to live in the Gospel stories, seeing them from the perspective of Jesus Christ. I have turned these stories over and over in my mind, meditating on the truth of each one, attempting to understand the mind of Christ. As I have tried to see with his eyes and hear with his ears, I have also tried to feel his motivation and know his heart.

When Jesus began his work on earth, he not only taught people by telling them what the Kingdom of God was all about, but also by showing them through his actions and interactions with others what it meant to live the Kingdom life. Jesus also issued a bold invitation for relationship. He made himself transparent and vulnerable, inviting the disciples to "come and see" and to follow him, knowing that behavior speaks the truth as nothing else. He revealed himself openly and completely to folks in the first century, and I believe he still reveals himself openly and completely to us today.

Enter into this process, using the God-given gift of imagination. No one of us will ever fully plumb the depths of the heart of Christ, nor can we know fully the mind of Christ, but in striving for that, we will surely become more like him than if we didn't try.

Although he was not privileged to walk, talk, and live with Jesus of Nazareth, Paul the Apostle knew the Living Christ intimately and exhorted us to "let the same mind be in you that was in Christ Jesus" (Phil 2:5). Paul also told us that the way to transformation is through the renewing of our minds (Rom 12:2). Exploring the words and actions of Jesus and identifying personally with him cannot fail to bring about some measure of transformation and renewal.

The writer of the Fourth Gospel, quoting Jesus, wrote that eternal life is knowing the one true God and knowing Christ (John 17:3). If Jesus prayed that his disciples would know him, it must be possible to do so. If Jesus issued the invitation to "come and follow," perhaps the method of *ChristHeart* is one way to know him.

KNOW MY PURPOSE

When did Jesus know that he was the Son of God? Did he know from the beginning of his life, as some have believed, that he was the Messiah, or was his recognition of his call an evolving understanding? How did Jesus reconcile his human nature with his divine nature? Did he have a choice as to whether or not he would fulfill his purpose in life? Did he ever want to be just an ordinary man? If it is true that Jesus was tempted in every way as we are, does this mean he wrestled with who he was and what he was supposed to do with his life?

In those long years he worked in the carpenter's shop—sanding, carving, and cleaning up the shavings from a long day's work—did Jesus question God, his heavenly father, about his role in life? How could he have done this if he were God?

In the following meditations I invite you to enter fully into Jesus' life as he grappled with who he was, as truly divine and truly human. Move into the Scriptures with an open heart to understand more clearly what it must have been like for God to take on human form, living, walking, and talking among people. For a few moments suspend your need to have your answers all wrapped up; be willing not to know the answers about who Jesus was in order to know Christ more fully. As you explore the purpose of Jesus in history, open your heart and mind to his purpose for your own life.

AWAKENING
The Boy Jesus in the Temple

Luke 2:41-52

Day 1
Luke 2:41-52

In your mind's eye imagine you are the young boy Jesus walking through the crowd at the Temple in Jerusalem. You make your way through the noisy throng, stopping to watch a Jewish pilgrim buy a bird or a lamb for a sacrifice. You inhale deeply the aromas of people, animals, and springtime.

Your eyes are accustomed to the gentle hills of Nazareth. You stare with wonder at the grandeur of the Temple. You walk through the various sections of the Temple, pausing to touch the stone walls and columns. What were the people like, you wonder, who laid these stones in place and raised the magnificent columns? You recall the stories of the building of the Temple.

Now and then a child darts across your path. You wonder if other boys your age sense the significance of being in this sacred place. You search for your friend from Nazareth to see if he, too, is caught up in the power of this sacred place.

For some reason you don't understand, you feel connected to a rich and powerful history more than ever before. Suddenly, what you have learned about your history takes on a deeper and more personal meaning for you. What is it about this particular visit to the Temple that is different from previous visits? Why are you seeing things you have never seen before?

Recall your own spiritual heritage and the most signifi-cant events of your life. How was God present with you in those events?

Day 2

Luke 2:41-52

Imagine what it was like to have been the boy Jesus observing the sacrifice of animals in the Temple at the Feast of the Passover. Experience with the preadolescent how it must have been to watch the blood from the sacrifices running freely through the troughs. With his eyes, see animal after animal slain at the hands of the priests.

As that twelve-year-old boy, walk down the corridors where the booths are. Watch humble Jewish peasants pay too much for animals to be sacrificed. Look in the eye of a hawker when he laughs with his son about the big price he is getting from the country folks. Notice how you feel when the hawker looks at you and then, guilty, looks away from your penetrating gaze.

You know that what is going on does not fit with what you have learned about your father. All of the slain animals in Jerusalem cannot bridge the gap between your father and the worshipers. These people have the wrong idea about who your father is.

Suddenly, it is as if the whole world opens up and you see things as you have never seen them before. Your whole body is charged with excitement and energy. You must tell the people that God does not want slain animals, that God wants their love. Quickly you make your way to the court where the rabbis are discussing the finer points of the Law.

Recall a time in your childhood or youth when you had an "awakening" or an "aha!" moment, when you knew that you would never see the world in the same light again. How was life different for you? What choices did you make because of that awakenings?

5

Day 3

Luke 2

Again imagine yourself as the young boy Jesus. As you sit in the crowded room with other seekers, listening to the teachers talk about the Law, your mind is whirling.

You remember the things your mother has told you about your birth and your unique relationship with the Heavenly Father. You recall the stories she has told you about taking you to the Temple when you were only eight days old. You think about all you have been taught about the long-expected Messiah.

You recall the words the old man, Simeon, said when he took you in his arms. Mary has repeated them to you so often, you know them by memory, and now you repeat them to yourself silently, your lips barely moving. Sometimes you wondered why Mary kept telling you about your birth.

In this moment all the pieces begin to fit together. For the first time your past has meaning; your history informs the present. With new insight you understand who you are and what your mission in life is to be. You are grasped by a call to be the person God created.

The sounds of the voices pierce your attention. You listen to the debate going on in the room. Voices rise and fall. You smile when an argument breaks out and one of the teachers storms out of the room. If only they could see as you see.

Think of a time when you have perceived something that others around you did not see. What was that experience like?

Day 4

Luke 2:41-52

Picture yourself as a young Jewish boy seated in the hall of respected and revered rabbis. Hear their voices and see their gestures as they debate the finer points of the Law.

Now see yourself rising to your feet. Hear yourself asking a question, interrupting the flow of debate among the adults. Watch as all heads turn in your direction and all eyes look you over. How does it feel to enter into their debate?

Imagine what it is like when the teachers take you seriously. Feel your delight when they honor your questions. Sense your excitement grow as they talk about your unusual understanding.

You know that they have dealt with precocious lads before. You aren't the first bold young man to challenge their positions. Jewish rabbis encourage questioning and value a strong intellect and a firm educational foundation.

Do they, however, sense something different in you? There is a power in your mind you hadn't experienced until this moment, a reasoning with depth that somehow seems intimately connected with God. You know, even if you don't understand how you know, that there is something beyond and above the Law the rabbis revere.

One question leads to another. One insight unfolds to reveal a deeper one. Your boldness increases. You thrill with the adventure of discovery of who you are and who God is.

As a youth, did you ever question or challenge a teacher or authority figure. How did his or her response shape your faith journey?

7

Day 5
Luke 2:41-52

Return again to the Temple courts where you, the young Jesus, have been questioning the rabbis for three days.

"Jesus!"

You are listening so intently to the rabbi that the voice of your parents barely penetrates your consciousness. When they call your name more forcefully, you turn in their direction.

"What are you doing?" they ask you. Are they angry with you? Suddenly you know what you have done. You see the worry on their faces. Yet, while you are sorry for having worried them, you know that you have passed from your childhood into a new phase of responsibility and accountability. You know that no matter what your relationship with your parents has been in the past, for you, everything is different.

Hear the anxiety in your mother's voice as she asks you why you have treated them in such a way. Watch yourself look into her eyes, knowing that she and Joseph have been the source of authority for you all of your life, but from this point on, you will be answering to a higher authority.

Gradually, God has revealed the divine plan for your life and mission. As your human development has progressed, your spiritual development also has matured. Now you must let go of childhood dependency and begin a new chapter.

Are there childhood dependencies you cling to even now? In what area of your life is God calling you to a greater maturity?

Day 6
Luke 2:41-52

Right there in the Temple, it is grow-up time for Jesus. Put yourself in his place, there with your mother and earthly father. In front of the authorities and teachers, you stand face to face with the people who have cared for you and nurtured you all of your life. These are the human instruments who have protected and taught you, guided and guarded you.

Look into Mary's eyes. Recall the stories you have heard about all she went through to give birth to you. Sense the special connection a Jewish lad has with his mother, a connection of mutual need-meeting. Recall her tender care for you and the love she has lavished on you all of your life. Her gentle, firm admonitions ring in your ears even now.

Look into Joseph's eyes. You look at his hands and think about the times he has taught you the best way to carve an ox-yoke or smooth a piece of furniture. Those same hands have lifted you up to pick the fruit on the highest branch and have pointed the way on the paths of Galilee.

Feel yourself stand up a little straighter, squaring your shoulders. Lift your head and look straight into your mother's eyes. Hear your voice, firm and clear, asking your parents the question that will change their lives and yours: "Don't you know I have to be about my father's business?"

To whom must you be willing to declare, "I must be about my father's business"? For you, what is that business?

9

Day 7
Luke 2:41-52

Imagine yourself as the young lad Jesus at home. You go about your days doing what growing and changing Jewish young men do. You work alongside Joseph in the carpentry shop. You study and learn. You obey your parents and the Jewish law.

All the time, though, the wider world lingers in the background of your mind. Always, the epiphany you experienced in the Temple in Jerusalem echoes in your heart, and there are times when you think you cannot sand wood another day.

Imagine yourself, at the end of a day, looking at the sunset. Standing outside your home, leaning up against the rough stone wall, you know that what is here in Nazareth is not all there is for you. Sometimes you are impatient to begin the business of your father. His world calls to you.

Growing through the restlessness of youth, you know that you are in training. The instructions of your father become clearer, and you know that just as your birth happened in the fullness of time, so will the time of your lifework.

Feel the gentle touch of Mary's hand on your shoulder. Turn and look into her eyes. Through the years, as the two of you have talked, both of you have grown in your understanding of what the Father wants of you. You know that God will give you the grace to wait.

Perhaps God has called you to a particular task, but your training period is longer than you had ever dreamed it would be. Is the wait preparing you for the next phase of your own call?

SETTING OUT

Jesus' Baptism

Matthew 3:13-17
Mark 1:2-11
Luke 3:21-22

Day 1
Matthew 3:13-17

Imagine yourself as Jesus, leaving what has been your home in Nazareth for thirty years. See yourself standing at the door, telling your mother, father, and brothers goodbye. Picture the expressions on their faces. Hear their parting words to you.

Feel your arms as you reach for your mother and embrace her. You tell her that the years of preparation have come to an end and it is time for you to do your heavenly father's business.

As you walk away from your boyhood home, memories tumble over each other in your mind. You recall the sounds of family life and the aromas of your mother's cooking. You hear Joseph's voice, teaching you the intricacies of woodworking. You look at your hands and can feel the various woods against your skin.

You look back and wave to Mary. You know that things will never be the same for either of you. Both of you will be changed when you return to her hearth again.

Finally, you cannot see her, but you walk on into your future. Your heart is full of emotion. You weep with thanksgiving for all you have had in that simple, loving home. You grieve because you know that leaving home is a kind of death. You walk on because the old must die in order for the new to be born.

Recall those moments in your own history when you had to walk away from that which you had outgrown. When have you had to let someone go? How did God comfort you in your letting go?

Day 2
Matthew 3:13-17

Today put yourself in the position of Jesus as a traveler, walking the dusty roads from Nazareth to the Jordan River. Look down at your feet as you make each deliberate, purposeful step. Feel the warmth of the sun and the breeze on your face.

As you walk, you turn over your life history in your mind. You recall the moments when your heavenly father has communicated His intent and purpose to you. You ponder how your understanding of who you are, as God's son, has grown as you have developed through childhood, adolescence, and early manhood.

Watch yourself take a break, sitting down beside the Jordan River. See yourself lean over the stream, splashing water on your face with your hands. Observe your reflection in the water. Ponder the significance of your new beginning.

As you sit beside the river, you hear the voice of your father, urging you to make your way down the river to the place where your cousin John is baptizing. The nudging guidance of your father continues, and you know what His will is.

See yourself stand up and begin walking toward the direction of voices. The thing you are most sure of is that God has asked you to take this remarkable action. You know that it will mark your new beginning and shape the form your ministry is going to take.

Recall a time in your life when you knew that God had guided you to do something that defied common sense or common custom. How did you know it was God guiding you?

13

Day 3

Matthew 3:13-17

Today picture yourself standing a few yards from John the Baptist. Watch him as he baptizes several people. Observe them as they come up out of the water; see their expressions.

See your rough cousin walk out of the water. Hear him urging the people who have not been baptized to repent of their sins. Notice the insistent tone in his voice.

Feel your feet begin to move in John's direction. What is the expression on his face when he sees you approaching? What does he do? What does he say to you?

You walk boldly toward your cousin. With each step you become more convinced that you are doing the will of your father. When you approach John, you meet him eye to eye and make your request directly and simply.

Hear the hush fall over the crowd. While you are fully aware of everyone's response to you, you know that you are guided by the one who sent you, and you trust His sense of timing. You are also keenly aware of John's reactions.

By being baptized, you want to underscore the deep, pervasive need for God that each person has. You want to demonstrate the necessity of humility and repentance. More than anything, you want your life to be a living, breathing picture of a will surrendered to the Father. You want others to see what it means to live in an unhindered love relationship with God.

Recall a time when you felt that you were fully surrendered to the will of God and pliable to God's guidance. What happened as a result of your obedience

Day 4

Matthew 3:13-17; Mark 1:2-11

Put yourself in Jesus' place as he made his request for baptism. See the look of shock play across John's face. After all, this isn't what he had expected. Hear the firmness in your voice as you insist that he do what you have asked of him.

Hear John's protests. Remember that John, created with free will, has a choice to make. You know that as strong-willed and bold as he is, he could refuse to baptize you.

As Jesus, you look deep into John's eyes and recognize the moment when John acknowledges that he, too, must obey the will of your father. You see a flicker of understanding in his eyes as he comes to terms with the fact of who you are. You watch the muscles along his jawline tremble. It seems that he struggles to keep his emotions under control

Your eyes are locked with John's. You begin walking toward the river. Feel the earth beneath your feet as it slopes down to meet the water. Watch as John begins to move alongside you. Imagine yourself walking down into the Jordan River with your cousin in the presence of speechless witnesses.

What is it like to enlist another human being in an important act of obedience to God's will? What are the risks? What are the rewards?

Day 5
Matthew 3:13-17; Luke 3:21-22

Imagine yourself as Jesus, walking down into the water with John. Notice every step you take. Be aware of every sensation. Feel the water as it encompasses your body and the riverbed beneath your feet. What is the temperature of the water? What sounds do you hear as you move through the water?

You look back at the faces of the people watching you on the bank of the river. You realize that your action is making a profound statement to them; some will understand, and others will not. More and more you move your awareness into the inner kingdom where you and your father meet in perfect unity.

Feel John's presence at your side. Feel the touch of his hand on your shoulder. You are aware of the power in John. You recall happy childhood memories of the two of you playing together as young boys. You notice your own hands and arms, crossing on your chest, in a picture of surrender to the will of your father.

You listen to John's prayer for you. You feel the strength in his body as he lowers your body down into the water, slowly and gently. You feel the water rush up around your shoulders and then your face. Finally, for a few seconds, you are totally submerged in the water, held by the powerful arms and hands of John. Then, as John raises you out of the river and you feel the water rushing down your face and arms, you pause to mark the significance of the moment.

Remember your own baptism. What is it like for you to know that Jesus experienced baptism, too?

Day 6
Matthew 3:13-17

Return to the moment when you, as Jesus, came up out of the baptismal waters of the Jordan River. Picture yourself moving up out of the water. See yourself pause as your father suddently reveals Himself to you in such a way that you know without a doubt you have done what He asked. You catch your breath.

As you look toward the heavens, you see them open. Watch as a dove moves toward you on the breath of God, the wind. You watch as the dove rests on your shoulder, knowing it is a sign from God. Your father is confirming your mission to you.

Then you hear your father's voice. Imagine hearing the voice of God telling you that you are His beloved son. Imagine what it is like to hear God use the very words that have been used in coronations of the kings for centuries.

As you stand there in that holy moment of unbroken communication with the Father, He completes the blessing, "in whom I am well pleased." You know that the Father is calling you to be the Messiah but that you will also be a suffering servant.

Stand there at the river and let the presence of God fill every cell of your body. Feel God's delight in who you are. Fully absorb the Father's confirmation of your mission.

How long has it been since you have experienced the full impact of God's pleasure in who you are as His beloved child? What prevents the constant assurance of God's delight in you?

Day 7
Matthew 3:13-17

If you had been Jesus, would you have taken time to talk to the people who witnessed your baptism? Would you have explained why you asked to be baptized by John? Would you try to justify your decision to participate in an act of repentance?

If you had been Jesus, would you have given the details of your earthly mission? Would you have verbalized your mission statement and then issued a call for confirmation?

Picture yourself as Jesus, walking away from the crowd. So moved were you by the moment of direct communication with the Father that you must go into solitude to process the experience.

See yourself walking along the river, totally absorbed in your thoughts and in God's love for you. The full impact of what your father has asked you to do is looming in your mind and heart.

You ponder the cost. You know that it would be far easier to be a king than a servant. You know that you could draw a lot more people into a popular movement of political power or military might than you can by the way of service. You realize that a conqueror is more politically correct than a loving servant.

As you walk, though, you know that you cannot be anything other than what the Father wills for you. You know that God's way is perfect and right and that you can trust God with all that concerns you. God's will is the way of forgiveness, mercy, love, and grace—the way that leads to joy and peace.

Recall the times when you have been sure of God's love for you. Do you act differently when you are sure of His love for you?

THE TEMPTATION
Setting Priorities

Matthew 4:1-11
Luke 4:1-13

Day 1
Matthew 4:1-11; Luke 4:1-13

How often mountaintop experiences are followed by valley experiences. Following a serious commitment to a particular call, a surrender of one's will and life to God, or a decision to take the high road, it is almost a guarantee that there will be a period of testing.

Imagine yourself as Jesus, following his public baptism. Remember the feeling of receiving your father's affirmation of your decision and call. Recall the warmth of God's presence in that moment of obedience.

Picture yourself walking toward the wilderness, away from the crowd. You are absorbed in your thoughts. The magnitude of your decision and the enormity of your task fill your mind. Your love for your heavenly father and your desire to please Him fill your heart.

You know that this is a transition time. Your old way of life is fading away, but the new is not yet fully formed. You know that you will never be the same again, but you don't know precisely what lies ahead for you.

Exactly how will you carry out your father's will? What will you do? Who will join you in your task?

Recall the time when you committed your life to God. Remember the times when you have been filled with the Holy Spirit of God. What experiences or decisions led to those holy moments?

Day 2
Luke 4:1-13

Picture yourself as Jesus, led by the Spirit into the wilderness. Look around you and see the desolation of the place. Feel the wind blow sand across your face. Hear the awesome sounds of silence.

Imagine yourself going without food for forty days. Imagine the hunger pangs. Feel the ache in your body as you try to rest on the hard ground. This is a wrestling time, a time for determining just how you will go about your ministry. This is when you will set your priorities. You are deciding how you will use your power.

Experience the intensity of praying as you sort out what it means to live surrendered to God, totally available to God for His will. As you live in the solitude of the wilderness, you think about how this new era in your life will rearrange all of your relationships, relationships that are important to you. From now on, your priorities are God's priorities. Feel the aloneness out there in the wilderness.

You are at a crossroads. You know that you are being tested. All of your desires, feelings, plans, and dreams must now be surrendered to God. You and God are beginning a new thing and moving toward a new level of intimacy.

Do you feel any fear? Do you have any doubts? As the human Jesus, do you question yourself or God? Do you have a choice? What are you giving up?

If you were to "sell out" to God, what would that mean for you?

Day 3

Luke 4:1-13

Using your imagination, create the scene of the confrontation between the devil and Jesus. Put yourself in Jesus' place, facing off with the power of evil that would ask him to be less and do less than he was created to be and do. Feel the intensity of this power struggle between the forces of evil and ultimate good.

Hear the challenge of the devil as he preys on your physical hunger and weakness. Hear the taunting of his voice as he addresses basic human need.

Imagine yourself as Jesus, knowing that you have, indeed, the power to turn any rock into bread, and that, in your work, you could meet the physical needs of people. You could draw people to you by satisfying their most basic survival needs. You could even make them dependent on you for their daily bread, so they would keep coming back to you. You know, however, that you could focus on primal hunger and never direct people to the bread of life that would satisfy their deepest cravings.

Is it a struggle for you, Jesus? Look into the face of evil and know that if you succumb, evil will think it has won.

You reach back into your memory and retrieve the words of your forefathers. You speak up, boldly and clearly, quoting Holy Scripture to meet the challenge of the evil one.

You have stood up to the test; you hope the testing is over.

Recall a time when you did not take the easy way out. What made you choose the way of strength?

Day 4

Luke 4:1-13

If you had been Jesus, would you have wondered why you were having to go through such a severe testing of your call? Why didn't your heavenly father spare you these confrontations with the devil and protect you, His son, from this?

Put yourself back in the wilderness scene. Imagine how you, as Jesus, felt when the devil appears one more time. What do you think when you hear the sly, seductive voice of the evil one, preying on you one more time with his cunning plans?

Hear the arrogance in the devil's voice as he offers what is not his to give: ultimate power and authority. Hear him make claims that are not his to make, promises he cannot keep, deals he cannot fulfill. Notice the sickening grip in your stomach as you look into the face of the Liar.

You square off with the devil one more time. You know that he does not have ultimate power to give. The power that has been granted to you by your father has been given to serve humankind rather than gain domination over them. Once again you call on Holy Scriptures to set things straight.

Hear the power in your voice as you set things straight with the evil one and proclaim the sovereignty of God. Feel the strength of God permeate your mind and body as you stand up to evil. Imagine yourself being filled with renewed stamina as you take your stand against the force of destruction.

Recall a time when you were empowered by God to stand up to the force of evil. What was the one thing that helped you do the right thing?

Day 5

Luke 4:1-13

Tests are over when they are over, even for Jesus. Temptations are finished when they are finished, even for Jesus.

Imagine yourself, having stood up to the devil, meeting him again. Imagine yourself in conversation with the devil about how you will do you work. Hear the devil teasing you with how it could be if you appealed to peoples' attraction to the spectacular and sensational. He wants you to give people a buzz, to thrill and excite them, and then hold your power over them. The only problem is that after people feel initial excitement, they need more and more excitement to get the same buzz.

What do you feel, up against the devil's temptations one more time? Didn't you put it straight with him the last time he tested you? Why must you keep dealing with him?

Hear the power in your voice as you set things straight one more time. Claiming the power of your heavenly father, you resist the temptation to appeal to peoples' need for entertainment. You make your decision to meet peoples' need for God. You declare the ultimate power of God. You let the devil know that God does not act on your terms, but on God's.

As you stare into the face of evil, you tell yourself, "Greater is he that is in me than he that is in the world."

Remember a time when God gave you the strength to stand up to the power of evil. Where do you need that strength now?

Day 6
Luke 4:1-13

Imagine yourself today as Jesus, having stood up to the power of evil. For the moment, anyway, the devil has abandoned you. For now, he is not in your face, taunting and teasing you, haunting you and hounding you with alternate plans, easy ways out, quick solutions, and easy answers to basic human needs. He isn't there, hassling you with other ways to do your work, ways that might appeal to peoples' immediate need, but not to their long-term need for God.

Feel the exhaustion of the battle. You have been tested. Your call has been challenged. Your way of doing your father's work has been called into question.

Feel the fatigue of the test. Weary, hungry, thirsty, and alone, you sit in the wilderness, pondering your future.

Remember your baptism as you sit there. Recall the exhilaration of that high and holy moment. Put the experience in the context of this most recent experience.

Did you know, as you walked away from the Jordan River, what lay ahead? If you had known the battle that was to be yours, would you have taken a different route? What does the future hold for you as you venture out into your work?

This one thing you know: whatever the future holds, you are different because of what you have experienced in the wilderness.

In what ways is God asking you to become clear about your own call?

Day 7

Luke 4:1-13

In this last meditation on the temptation of Jesus, focus on the moment when he had stood up to the force of evil. Feel with him the relief of the moment when evil has fled.

For now the battle is over, and God and you have won. You know that you will do your work as your father wills, and you will not succumb to seducing people into following you. You will draw people to God and not to a momentary experience. You will not entertain them; you will point them beyond yourself to God, who meets all needs. You will show them the way to the only real power, the power of the one true God.

As you sit there, hear the quietness of the moment, the utter stillness of solitude. You are weary, but there is a clarity in your mind that is like a cloudless, blue sky. You sense the still, small voice of your father.

Suddenly, you look up and see an angel, a messenger from your father. Allow the angel to meet your physical needs of hunger and thirst. Receive the gifts of solace and comfort from the angel as gifts from your father. Know that the presence of the ministering angel is the blessing of your father, the blessing that follows meeting the tests.

Feel relief course through your veins. Feel yourself relax into the blessing of your father. Give thanks for His provision.

When have you stood up to evil? When has God sent ministering angels to meet you at the point of your need?

BEGINNING THE ADVENTURE
Jesus' Mission Statement

Matthew 4:18-22
Mark 1:16-20
Luke 4:14-30: 5:1-11
John 1:35-42

Day 1
Luke 4:14-30

How long did Jesus take to recover from the strenuous experience in the wilderness? Did he return home to his family to rest and clean up? Or did he move immediately into his lifework, exhilarated by the experience of testing in the wilderness?

See him in your imagination as he returned to Galilee, filled with the power of the Spirit, ready for his task. Feel with him as he went about teaching and preaching. Wherever he went, the news about him spread.

Imagine him at the end of a day, taking stock of his new work and the responses of the people with him. Feel his inner conviction grow as the people eagerly welcome his good news. Experience his satisfaction as he connects with people heart to heart.

Ponder how it must have felt for Jesus, knowing he was on the right track, doing what he was supposed to be doing. Imagine the satisfaction and gratification of knowing that what you are doing is pleasing to your heavenly father and also meets human needs.

Your course is set. You've made your decisions, and you feel the strength that follows commitment.

In what areas of life do you know that you are doing the right thing? How does it feel to you when you please God?

Day 2
Luke 4:14-30

Put yourself in the place of Jesus on a Sabbath. See yourself walking into Nazareth, your hometown. Here and there you greet a friend. A relative calls out to you from across the way, and you wave. A neighbor stops to tell you about her child, and you stop and listen with your heart.

You move deliberately toward the synagogue, the place you have been going all of your life. You move eagerly up the steps. You can hardly wait to see your teachers and tell them about what has happened to you.

You move into the sacred space with confidence, for these are your people, your kinsmen. These are the people who have taught and guided you. Will they realize how prophecy is being fulfilled in your teaching? Have they heard about your baptism and your experience in the wilderness? What do they know about the teaching you have been doing? Do they approve? Are they proud of you? Will they want you to share your experiences with them?

How do the people respond to you now? When you look into their eyes, do you see openness or reserve? Are they threatened by you, or do you welcome the new? Are they ready to hear what you have to say? Do they want to hear from you?

What is it like for you when you return home after a mountaintop experience with God? Who really wants to hear how it was on the mountaintop and how you've changed?

Day 3
Luke 4:14-30

Using the power of imagination, hear the silence in the synagogue when you, as Jesus, get up to read. See the room with all eyes focused on you. Perhaps your heart is beating so rapidly, you think they can hear it. Your palms may be sweaty, but you know this is a defining moment, so you proceed.

You look up, and the leader is handing you the sacred scroll. Look into his eyes. What do you see? Are they welcoming eyes? Do they sense a new power in you?

Feel the weight of the scroll in your hands. Imagine yourself unrolling it to the text you can quote by heart, a text that is emblazoned on your mind.

You take a deep breath, and then you quote the beloved words. You don't have to read, but you hold the scroll up, giving it the respect that sacred scripture deserves. As the words roll off your tongue, you look around at the faces of your family of faith.

Hear the strength of your voice grow as you proclaim your mission statement. Hear your voice, firm and forceful, as you announce your plans for your work. Feel the excitement grow in your heart until you think it will burst, excitement over the lives that will be changed by the good news of the Living God. What power there is in the will of God! How exhilarating it is to be right in the middle of that will!

Have you written your mission statement? Is it consistent with the heart of Christ?

Day 4
Luke 4:20-30

Pick up the scene from yesterday, the scene in the synagogue when you, as Jesus, used scripture to declare your mission statement. Imagine yourself standing before the religious leaders, having made your statement. Hear the hush in the room.

See yourself rolling up the scroll and handing it to the attendant. The silence in the room is deafening.

You cannot imagine that these people, your family of faith, would not welcome your new mission with gladness. You can't imagine that they would ever question you. After all, they have known you all of your life. Surely they, of all people, know your heart. They will see how right this is. These, your people and your teachers, will affirm your call.

You sit down. Everyone is staring at you, so you make a bold statement about the fulfillment of the prophecy. If you use scripture, especially the prophet Isaiah, they will have confidence in what you are doing.

The people begin to speak well of you, and you feel the thrill of their approval. You hear some murmurings about your heritage as Joseph's son, so you respond by bringing in a little more Jewish history to undergird your message, but apparently you go too far. Suddenly the mood changes, and those who have known you all of your life turn on you.

The most severe tests of faith are often within the context of one's own family. How does your family help or hinder your call?

Day 5
John 1:35-42

Where would you have gone to find disciples if you had been Jesus? Would you have sought out people you had known for a long time, or would you simply have looked for open minds and hearts? Would you have asked for an application and references, or would you have found individuals who were open to the generosity of God's spirit, people who were willing to take risks and explore new ways of living with God in the world?

Imagine yourself, as Jesus, walking down the street in one of the little villages of Galilee. See the clear, blue sky overhead. Hear the song of a bird, the laughter of children, the swoosh of a housewife's broom. Pause to get a drink of water. Buy a piece of fruit and taste its goodness.

Thoughts are turning over in your mind as you exchange greetings. You are aware of people following you, and you respond to people who want to engage you in dialogue. You are, however, still stinging from the rejection in your hometown, so you know that you must discern carefully whom you will call to be a part of your inner circle.

You are aware that someone is following you. You pause, and the person stops. You turn around. You look into the eyes of this stranger. "What do you want?" you ask him, for you know that desire and motivation are of prime importance.

What would you answer if Jesus were to ask you, "What do you want?" What do you really want?

Day 6
Matthew 4:18-22; Mark 1:16-20

Imagine what thoughts Jesus had as he chose his disciples. What were his criteria? Did he agonize over each choice, or did he know quickly, as he listened to the guidance of his father, who would work best within the inner circle?

Who could be entrusted with the most precious truths of all? Who could be counted on to be prudent and careful with the gems of life-changing wisdom? What strengths and character traits would work best together? Did education matter, or was it simply a matter of a heart that was humble enough to receive the good news?

As Jesus, watch yourself moving about the villages of Galilee, selecting your team. See yourself making your choices and extending your invitations. Notice how you look into the eyes of each person, gauging their reactions and judging their readiness to be a part of a history-changing endeavor.

You invite these potential disciples to come and follow you around, to test you and see if your walk matches your talk. You invite them to observe you up close; you are willing to be transparent and vulnerable, to let them really know you. Then they can decide if what you say really means anything.

How open are you to letting people see you up close? Who has made herself vulnerable to you? Who has been your best teacher? Did his walk match his talk?

Day 7
Luke 5:1-11

Use your imagination to paint the picture of Jesus, teaching from the boat on the lake. Hear the lapping of the water against the shore. Feel the breeze on your face. Watch the upturned faces as people listen attentively to your teaching.

You notice the fisherman Simon. You have been watching him for quite some time. You call out instructions to him about fishing. You, a carpenter, are telling Simon how to fish. (Or are you testing him to see if he is humble enough to follow instructions?)

Simon argues with you, but then he does what you suggested. You watch with satisfaction as he brings up the biggest catch of his fishing career. You laugh with ecstasy as you watch him haul in his catch, so many fish that he has to call for help. You sit back in your boat and enjoy the spectacle of the catch.

You get out of your boat and begin to walk up the hill. Suddenly, Simon runs up to you and falls down on his knees. When you look into his face, you see an unformed man with an open heart. You see untapped strength and unrealized potential. You see the possibility of an able disciple. You see—at least you think you see—a good friend.

In that moment of encounter your destiny and Simon Peter's meet. It is a life-changing moment, and you know it.

If Jesus could look into your face today, what untapped strength and unrealized potential would he see?

INVITATION
Jesus' Plea to All Humankind

Matthew 11:28-30

Day 1
Matthew 11:28-30

Put yourself in the shoes of Jesus of Nazareth. You have been baptized in the Jordan River by your cousin John. You have gone through the testing in the wilderness and have taken your stand concerning the shape of your ministry. You have selected a group of twelve men as your disciples, or disciplined learners. You have spent hours talking with them, clarifying what it means for them to be in relationship with your heavenly father.

Your mission is to help them understand the kingdom of God and what that means to their everyday lives. You are the best picture of God they can have, and it is up to you to communicate the love and power of your heavenly father.

Imagine having healed a man with leprosy and then discussing what you have done with these disciples. See yourself trying to interpret the healing of the paralytic to these amazed men. Try to picture yourself explaining the power that is in you. How would you describe to Andrew and Thomas the difference between your message and that of the Pharisees?

You know what it is like to explain something new and different. You understand the basic human resistance to that which challenges the status quo. You have asked your disciples to go against the grain of all they have believed. Look into the eyes of each man and see what each must do in order to know you. You have great compassion for them.

How would you explain the kingdom of God to your friends?

Day 2
Matthew 11:28-30

Using the God-given gift of imagination, picture yourself as Jesus, walking through the dusty streets of Jerusalem. You have given your disciples a huge assignment.

Like any teacher, you wonder if they fully understand what you have said to them. Their task will tax them to the end of their abilities, but the adequacy of God will meet them.

As you look at their faces, your heart wrenches. You know how costly it is will be for them to follow you. You can see how it will be when they start confronting the power bases and challenging the status quo. Your experience so far has shown how hard it is for human beings to bear unconditional love.

Now you look into the faces of these men whom you have come to love and while you know that they will have unbelievable challenges, you remember those who are bound by the weight of the law. You see in your memory the faces of those who are guilt-ridden. You weep for the ones who keep trying to atone for their own sin, for those who cannot pay a fine high enough to relieve themselves of the weight of their shame.

You think of all the ways you have seen people try to fix themselves and make themselves good enough. You recall all the false prophets who have made empty promises. Your heart goes out to all humankind. "Come to me!" you plead, knowing that only in you can there be true rest.

Recall a time when you had to watch someone you love struggle to grow up or become free. What was that experience like for you?

Day 3

Matthew 11:28-30

Again picture yourself as Jesus. You look into the eyes of the people around you and see straight to their inner beings. You know all the ways that people have tried to save themselves. It is your mission to show them a better way.

You look into the eyes of a mother, grieving for her lost child. You see a man whose body is racked with pain. Another young man whose life has consisted of one failure after another finds you. You see all the people who have tried to be good and make themselves right by keeping an unbearable number of laws.

Your father never intended for people to be broken by life and wearied by getting through the day. He never meant for His laws to break His children; He intended for His commandments to free them. More than anything you want each person to know the freedom of your love and to have the deep-seated peace that comes from resting in the Father's care.

"Come to me!" you tell them, knowing full well that some will be skeptical and others will think your invitation is arrogant and self-serving. But you invite them into relationship anyway.

"Come to me, all of you who are weary and burdened," you plead. Your heart aches for the burdens they carry. You want them to give you a chance to show them a better way of life. You plead with them to let you carry their burdens, but you know that all you can do is issue an invitation.

As you look into the eyes of people, do you see the burdens they carry? What about your own weariness?

Day 4
Matthew 11:28-30

On this day see yourself as Jesus again, milling among the crowds of people. How does it feel to speak to supporters and nonsupporters, thrill-seekers and truth-seekers?

Hear the compassion and yearning in your words. Imagine what it would have been like to have said, "I will give you the rest you need," to people who were trying to decide to trust you.

You cannot smooth away all the rough edges for people and still leave them their God-given gift of free choice. You aren't trying to take all their problems away from them.

You tell them there is a way to live with inner peace and harmony that makes the problems bearable. It is possible for them to have an inner freedom like they have never known before, even when appearances would indicate otherwise. The "rest" you are offering has to do with the security of being surrendered to the one who holds the resources of the world in His hands.

You look into the faces of those who have heard your invitation. You wonder if they will accept the invitation. You see a flicker of response here, a movement toward you there. Your promise will be backed up by action. You will put your life on the line to fulfill your word to those who accept your invitation.

Think of a time when you had some answers or advice that someone close to you needed. Remember what it was like, trying to convince them to do what was good for them. What is it like to offer a gift to someone who may or may not want it?

Day 5
Matthew 11:28-30

To understand the mind and heart of Jesus, the Son of God, picture yourself as the carpenter from Nazareth. You look out into the crowd, and then your attention is diverted. You see an ox over at the edge of the crowd, and it reminds you of the many ox yokes you have made in Joseph's shop.

Look down at your hands. Rub them together. Feel the rough callouses. So many pieces of wood have passed through those hands that you can almost feel the various forms. You smile when you think about how well the yokes you made fit the animals. You remember with pride that each yoke perfectly fit the animal for which it was made.

Suddenly you make a connection. These people will understand your imagery. They can relate to well-fitting yokes, so you urge them, "Take my yoke upon you and learn from me."

You know that they have put their necks in many yokes that chaffed and rubbed their skin. You have watched them stick their necks into the yoke of the law and be broken by the effort. You have seen your father's children with their necks in the yokes of other gods that were not worthy of a child of His, a child made in His image.

You know exactly what each one needs in order to become whole. You have the perfectly fitting yoke for each person. There's no one-size-fits-all for your followers.

What yokes keep you crippled? Addictions? Good works? Legalism? People-pleasing?

Day 6
Matthew 11:28-30

Jesus Christ, because he was in perfect union with his father, had access to unlimited power and force. He could turn water into wine and raise the dead. He could multiply food and walk on the water. Because he was God, all of creation was subordinate to him. In his invitation to the people, however, he described himself as gentle and humble in heart.

Visualize yourself as Jesus, knowing your power, and yet subordinating that power to the Father's purposes. Imagine what it must have felt like to have infinite strength, even though you described yourself as gentle and humble in heart. Imagine God limiting Himself.

As you picture yourself in the shoes of Jesus, try to imagine what it was like to accommodate yourself to the needs of the people because you loved them so much. See yourself wanting to reveal the full nature of your heavenly father to people who are weary and burdened.

You could, if you chose, instantly snatch their burdens from them. Instead you call them into relationship with you. You respect them so much that you honor the free will your father wrote into their very beings. To be true to who you are, you assume the nature of a gentle servant to them, inviting them into relationship and promising them rest. As Jesus, you set people free to know you or not to know you, to come to you or to turn away from you.

How do you think it affects Jesus to risk loving you?

Day 7
Matthew 11:28-30

Return in your mind's eye to the poignant moment when the invitation of Jesus rings out across the crowd. Picture yourself again as Jesus. Feel the longing in his heart to set people free. Get in touch with how it must have been for him to have opened himself up as he did, risking rejection or acceptance.

As you have come to understand the mind and heart of Jesus, you know that his intent is born out of pure love. Imagine your own heart filling, as his did, with tenderness for people.

As Jesus, watch someone walk away and then feel your heart break. You let her go, however, rather than make her stay. See a person wavering. You look him straight in the eye, pleading with him to surrender to joy and gladness, mercy and grace.

Now imagine that a straggler on the outside of the crowd suddenly starts toward you. Your heart lifts. Your eyes well with tears. You know that only you can give the person all she needs for an abundant life.

As she approaches you, your eyes are locked with hers. Feel your hands as you place them on her shoulders. Sense the hush of the crowd. Feel the expectancy as people wait to see what you will do. "My yoke is easy," you tell her, wanting her to know that whatever path the Heavenly Father has laid out for her will fit her perfectly. "My burden is light."

The Living Christ designs our journeys to fit perfectly. Where is Christ at work in your journey today?

KNOW WHO I AM

When God the Father wanted human beings to know who He was and what His nature was, He put on human flesh and showed humankind His character. When the Creator of all things wanted to reveal Himself to His children, God sent His son as a visible, tangible, real person with both a divine nature and a human nature. Jesus is the best picture of God that we have.

In his life on earth God the Son chose to make himself transparent and vulnerable. He revealed himself by living out in the open so that people could see him, touch him, and share life with him. Jesus was approachable and available to people. He drew near to them in order to share life at the deepest level possible.

Jesus was open about what he believed. He made no secret of his nature, but acted out his personhood under the microscope of village and family life. He did not try to protect himself. Confident in who he was, Jesus was never on the defensive.

When it was time for Jesus to begin his public ministry, he invited disciples into a close relationship with him. In that openness he made available to those whom he would lead the full range of his experience. Sharing his innermost thoughts, telling them about his struggles, and letting them see him being questioned and challenged, Jesus lived out his days and nights in such a way that it was possible for people to know him.

In the following meditations open your heart to the possibility of knowing more fully the human and divine Jesus.

A FIRST GLIMPSE OF GLORY

The Wedding at Cana

John 2:1-12

Day 1

John 2:11-12

Picture yourself on a warm spring night, attending a wedding party. In your mind's eye imagine you are Jesus, right in the middle of the action.

Hear the laughter and good wishes being tossed across the crowded room for the bride and groom. See the young couple, blushing and innocent. Watch your friends, celebrating and talking to each other in clusters gathered around the room.

You walk through the room. Pause to hug an old friend whom you haven't seen in a long time. Share a funny story with a cousin. Enjoy the succulent flavors at the banquet table.

Imagine that you walk over to the side of the room and lean against a doorframe. A fresh evening breeze brushes your face and stirs your clothing. You lean back against the wall and savor the warmth of belonging. These are your people. You have shared your life with them. It is with them that you have grown up. With them you have wept at funerals and rejoiced at weddings and birthings. With these men and women you have lived out the rhythms of work and play, worship and study. With them you have shared the sameness of daily routines.

Jesus didn't start loving people when he began his public ministry. He grew up in an atmosphere of love and belonging; he knew what it was to have close, personal relationships. How are you doing at loving the people closest to you?

Day 2
John 2:1-4

In your imagination place yourself back in that doorframe. Stretch your mind to try to see, hear, and feel what it was like to have been Jesus at the Jewish wedding.

Suddenly you feel a hand on your arm. Turning, you look straight into the eyes of Mary, your mother. Hear her voice tell you that the hosts have run out of wine. See the concern on her face as she looks toward the hosts and back at you.

The pressure of your mother's hand on your arm and the tone in her voice are nothing to compare with the unspoken push you sense coming from her heart to yours. Mary has nurtured you and cared for you all of your life. Yet both of you know that you must take your guidance from a higher authority.

Hear your voice as you ask her why she is involving you in this dilemma. Quietly, yet urgently, you explain to her that it isn't time for you to reveal your power. Explain to her that this isn't really the setting you had in mind for performing your first public miracle. Doing something about the wine would open up all sorts of things you aren't quite ready to face.

As her son, look into Mary's eyes. You and she share a history that no other human beings have shared. Your heavenly father has talked to her about you since before you were born. Perhaps there have been times when you have known that you were going to have to act on what God has called you to do.

What persons has God used to nudge you out of your comfort zone to do what you were created to do?

Day 3
John 2:1-5

As Jesus, stand with Mary in the doorway. The silence hangs heavy between you. You look into her eyes and recognize the firmness and strength you have known all through your childhood and adolescence. You remember how she stood by in your young adult years as a tower of fortitude and faith.

You can't believe your ears, though, when you hear Mary call the servants to her and tell them to follow your instructions. What does she think she is doing? Didn't she hear you when you told her you weren't ready to perform a miracle and that this wasn't really what you had in mind for tonight?

Thoughts tumble through your mind as you watch Mary walk away and into the crowd. Feelings about yourself and your role in the world wrestle with feelings about your mother and the hosts. You cast your eyes around the room, locating your disciples, and then you look back into the curious, waiting eyes of the servants.

Most important of all, through the roar of the festive crowd, you hear the clear, steady, unmistakable voice of your father. Within the recesses of your own mind and heart the voice of love grows stronger and surer, and with it comes the guidance and direction you need. With the voice of your father echoing in your mind and heart, you have complete clarity of thought and purpose. With the assurance of His indwelling presence, you know exactly what you are supposed to do and how to do it.

How do you discern when God's voice is calling you into action?

Day 4

John 2:1-7

Today, as Jesus, imagine yourself as a man with a job to do. Picture yourself looking into the eyes of the servants. What do you see in their faces? Will they cooperate, or will they balk? Will they participate with you in carrying out the will of the Heavenly Father, or will they try to sabotage His plans?

See yourself approach the six stone water jars used for ceremonial washing. You lean over and caress the rough surfaces with your hands. You tilt them and see that they are empty. Turn around and look at the servants who are watching you.

Now you know fully what you are to do. "Fill the jars with water," you tell the servants, authority and confidence in your voice. "Make sure you fill every one to the brim."

See the servants look at you with puzzlement on their faces. They don't question you. Somehow they must recognize authority in your voice. They move to carry out your instructions. You feel a tug in your heart as you watch the obedience of these faithful servants. You know that they don't understand, but they are willing to trust you. You know that they are bringing to you a simple, humble element—water. How many times in the future will you ask people simply to give you what they have and to obey you, whether or not they know what you are doing.

What simple, humble task might the Living Christ be asking you to do for him today? In what way is he asking you to obey and trust him?

Day 5

John 2:1-10

Picture yourself as Jesus, standing with the servants around the six stone pots filled with water. Imagine that you close your eyes and take a long, slow breath. Within the inner recesses of your heart and mind you are in direct communication with the Creator of the universe, the Maker of all that is. In that moment when you go into the inner kingdom, you are connecting at the most intimate level possible with your heavenly father. You are praying to Him, and He is praying to you. You and God are perfectly attuned to each other.

You open your eyes and look down at the water in the pots. In this moment every fiber of your being is charged with power and love. You are fully aware of everything that is going on in you and around you. You are fully alive, fully human, and fully divine.

Look into the faces of the servants, people who are willing to be instruments in the miracle. Tell them, quietly, to draw out some of the water and take it to the master of the banquet.

Step back, away from the stone pots, and watch the astonished servant dip down into the pot and bring up sparkling wine. Hear the excitement in his voice as he exclaims over the change in the humble water to the finest wine. Watch the master of the banquet taste the wine. See relief and amazement light his eyes when he realizes that neither he nor the bridegroom will be embarrassed because he has run out of wine.

The Living Christ wants to change water into wine for you. What do you need to do to cooperate with him?

Day 6
John 2:1-11

If you had been Jesus, what would you have done after you had turned the water into wine? Would you have stayed around and explained how you did it to satisfy the curious? Would you have repeated the miracle in case people hadn't understood? Would you have slipped quietly away to keep from making a scene?

Imagine yourself, as Jesus, walking away from the house where the merriment continued. Hear the sounds of the party fade away and the sounds of the night increase. Watch yourself walk over to a large rock and sit down. Look up at the moon. Feel the night air against your skin. Smell the freshness of the earth.

You know this moment will change everything in your life. From this point on, your days and nights will be different. Everyone—your family, friends, disciples, and even strangers —will relate to you differently now that you have manifested the power of your father in such a public way.

You wonder if people will want to be near you now for what you can do for them or simply because they love you. Will people understand that the miracles you perform are only for the purpose of glorifying your father and not for bringing attention to yourself? Will the disciples understand that the wonders you perform are to benefit persons and not to build a crowd or raise money for the treasury?

The Living Christ wants to transform your life. Do you want him for his presents or for his presence?

Day 7

The wedding party continues. The sounds of festive music and revelry drift across the night breezes. The aromas from the kitchen continue to fill the air.

See yourself looking into the eyes of your friends and knowing that now your friendship will take on a different tone. Hear the questions of the awe-struck men who had chosen to follow you, a Galilean carpenter.

See yourself standing with James, John, and Simon. Look into the eyes of Andrew and Phillip. Feel your hand reaching out to touch Nathanael's shoulder. You can't simply make small talk now. You can't act as if nothing has happened. You want to tell them everything, but where do you begin?

You sense a small figure walk up behind you and barely brush your sleeve. You turn and look down into the eyes of your mother. You see tears glistening in the corners of her eyes. One of them escapes and rolls down her soft cheek. Tenderly, you wipe it away with your finger.

Is that gratitude in your mother's eyes? Is that pride on Mary's face? She always has encouraged you and reminded you who you were and what you were to do. Is that sorrow mingled with joy in her eyes? You and she both know that tonight's miracle will change everything for the two of you.

Imagine what it was like for Jesus to move out of the warmth of his family and into the demands of his call. In what ways has the call of God in your life affected your closest relationships?

BEING FAMILY/BEING ONESELF
Jesus' Definition of the Family

Mark 3:1-44; 6:1-4

Day 1
Mark 3:1-19

Imagine yourself as Jesus the Teacher embarking on your day's tasks. You are eager to get out and about, to begin teaching and challenging people to new ways.

As you prepare to meet the new day, the ideas of truth and wisdom tumble over and over in your mind. You see the problems facing humankind, and you know that the truth you have learned from your father will make a difference in the way people live.

Imagine what it is like for Jesus to be bursting with eagerness to tell people about the ways of God. Imagine the fervor and passion that accompany the joy of learning and then passing on to another that which can change life. How must it feel to know the most precious truths that can set them free and make them whole?

Imagine Jesus' eagerness as he sets out on a new venture, a change in career, an exciting challenge. Recall the feeling of "bursting at the seams" when you cannot wait to share the good news you have discovered with someone else.

Imagine how it must be for Jesus when crowds follow him, demanding to hear more of the Good News. How does he feel when people seek him?

Do you have passion about your lifework? If not, why not?

Day 2
Mark 3:1-19

On this day "be with" Jesus as he makes his way from his homebase to the marketplace and synagogue. Walk with him from the warmth and security of home, family, and friends out into the center of the crowds.

Notice how one, and then another, joins Jesus as he makes his way through the city. Imagine what it is like for him to draw a crowd everywhere he goes. Does he ever wonder what makes certain people come to him while others stay away?

See him as he deals with the confrontations from the religious leaders and teachers. Imagine yourself meeting their challenges about fasting, healing, and the law. How do you feel going toe to toe with the authorities on important matters of faith and religious dogma?

Put yourself in the shoes of Jesus as he teaches the twelve members of his inner circle. It is one thing to speak to the crowds and teach the masses; it is quite another to impart truth to a small group, up close and personal.

Imagine yourself so filled with the Spirit of God that you teach with authority and courage. Feel the power of Jesus, the power of humility, and the power of being firmly connected with God. What is it like to be so intimately connected with the God of the universe that you can walk into any situation and know that you are doing what God the Father wants from you?

Are you confident that you are doing what God created you to do?

Day 3

Mark 3:20-44

On this day picture yourself in the home of a friend. You have gone there to share a meal with your disciples. Perhaps you have gone there to get away from the crowd. You may even want to take a nap.

Picture how the house looks. Smell the aroma of freshly baked bread. Taste the refreshing coolness of water. Feel the warmth of being with your close friends in the home of one who has welcomed you and shown you hospitality. Hear the sounds of laughter among people who know each other well.

Hear the chatter of people coming to the door, looking for you. Notice that strangers and acquaintances alike gather in the home of your friend, all because of you. As you look into their faces, you see yearning and longing in the eyes of some; on the other hand, you also see the eyes of curiosity-seekers. You know that people come to you with mixed motives, but you want to meet them all with the truth that will set them free.

What do you do? Do you long for a moment of peace and quiet? Are you embarrassed at the inconvenience you are causing your host? Are you pleased that people want to know more about your good news? Are you concerned at all about how your actions are affecting others?

Are you aware of how your actions affect your loved ones? What price do others pay to be your friend?

Day 4

Mark 3:20-44

Return to the scene in the friend's house. Attempt to see the crowd with the eyes of Jesus. Try to hear their questions with his ears. Look at the people with the heart of the Savior, a heart filled with love and compassion.

Suddenly you begin to hear that your family—your own family—thinks you are out of your mind. It is one thing for the religious authorities to question you, but it is quite another to be misunderstood by your own family. How can it be that the very ones with whom you have lived and loved for all of your life don't understand you?

How can it be that the people closest to you are questioning your motivation? Is it possible that they, the members of your family, are questioning your sanity? Don't they know you well enough to realize that you are fulfilling the purpose for which you were made? Do they doubt that you are, indeed, "being about your father's business?"

What do you do, given the doubts and concerns of your family? Do their doubts make you question yourself, or do they make you stronger? Do you feel a need to convince them of your mission and your sanity? Does the questioning of your family feel like betrayal?

What is it like for you when the call of God is at odds with your family? How do you know the difference between following the call of God and arrogance?

Day 5
Mark 3:20-44

As the human Jesus, you have grown up within the context of family life. You are a product of your culture. You have family loyalties that every other Jewish man has. You understand the mother/son, father/son dynamics. You have experienced life with siblings.

Standing in that room, teaching people who have sought you out, you carry the years of family and community life within your heart. You hold the memories of nights around the family table and holidays and festivals shared with family and friends. You have been a part of solving family problems and reaching family goals.

Far more forceful within you, however, is the conviction of your own call. How much you want to be who you are and who you were created to be and still hold on to your family connections. You want to fly with the wings of freedom, but you also want to retain your sense of rootedness within your family system.

You close your eyes and seek the guidance of your heavenly father, the one who set up this divine/human problem in the beginning. What does He have to say about this dilemma? How would He resolve your competing loyalties?

You know that you must follow the guidance of God. You know that God's rule and reign must triumph in your heart, mind, and will. You pray, as you surrender to God's will, that your family will understand and come along on the journey.

What does God say to you about balancing competing loyalties?

Day 6
Mark 3:31-35

Now and then there are defining moments in life, those moments when you make a choice or take a stand, and from that time on, life is different. For Jesus, there were several of those significant moments. During his life and work there were decisions he made when there was no turning back.

Put yourself in the shoes of Jesus. Imagine yourself standing before the crowd that has gathered to hear you teach. Feel the tension in the air when your family arrives to take you home. Experience the inner battle that occurs when you know that you must move forward into your own life and destiny, regardless of how it affects your family.

Hear your words as you set your course. Hear yourself broadening the concept of "family" to include those who are on the same journey as you. Hear yourself not alienating your own family members, but reaching out to embrace and include those who are willing to follow God.

Do you worry about how your mother and brothers will react to what you have done and what you say? What feeling is in your heart as you take your stand? Will they understand, or will they reject you? Are you, in fact, cutting the cords or widening the circle?

How well do you keep the balance between your life as an individual and your life within your family?

Day 7
Mark 6:1-4

Imagine yourself as Jesus, teaching in the synagogue. As you listen to the questions of your disciples and respond to them, you begin to hear comments that question you as a teacher. With the heart of Jesus, listen to those questions:

Who does he think he is?

He's just the carpenter's son. What could he know?

Even his sisters are offended by him. What is he doing making himself out to be a teacher?

What will your response be to the disdain of your fellow townspeople? After all, these are the people who have known you all your life.

Are you defensive? Do you feel the need to explain or rationalize your behavior?

Could they be right? Maybe you should just go back to the carpenter's bench and do what you've always done.

What is this doing to Mary, your mother? Does she still believe in you and your purpose, or has she bought into the doubt of the others?

Imagine the moment when you recognize, perhaps for the first time, the truth that those who have known you all your life may not be able to let you grow up into your mission.

In what area of your life do you feel most effective? Least effective?

WHO AM I TO YOU?

Jesus' Question to His Inner Circle

Matthew 16:13-16; 17:1-8

Day 1
Matthew 16:13-16

As Jesus, you have spent some time with the people who have signed on to be your disciples. You've been in constant dialogue with them. They have seen you healing, teaching, and preaching. They have watched you interact with others and observed your life of prayer.

You are aware that rumors about who you are have been floating in the air. You want to see how clear the disciples are about your true identity. Are they getting the message? Are they seeing you for who you really are, or are they still deluded or confused? Are their minds and hearts opening to the wider truth of God's purpose for you and them, or do they have limited vision?

See yourself sitting down, leaning against a tree. You and the disciples have been traveling for some time, and all of you need a break. Look around the circle of new friends. Realize what they have given up in order to follow you and learn from you. See them for who they are, bold and brave seekers, willing to take a risk with you.

Ask them, clearly and directly, what they are hearing about your identity. Watch their eyes. Observe their body language. Listen for the nonverbal meaning that will tell you much.

How well do you know who you really are? How well do your friends and loved ones know your true identity?

Day 2
Matthew 16:13-16

Re-create the outdoor scene in which Jesus and his disciples gathered under a tree to rest after a day of traveling. You, as Jesus, have been listening to the disciples talking about the effects you are having on people. You ask them to tell you what people have been saying about your identity. You listen to their responses.

Suddenly you know that they need to understand clearly who you are, if they can, so you ask them to tell you what they think. You want them to think for themselves. You want them to come to their own conclusions about who you are.

Hear the rustling of the wind as the significance of your question permeates their minds. They are thinking it over. You watch them as the wheels turn. As you look into their faces, you know that how they answer the question, "Who do you say that I am?" will determine everything for them. In fact, it is one of the most significant and life-changing questions they will ever face.

You wait. They think. They look at each other. You peer into each face. Some meet you eye to eye; others look down or toward the horizon.

Who will speak first? Will they agree about your identity? Do they really understand the significance of the question? Do they really understand how you can change their lives?

What is it like to be known for who you really are? What is it like to know Jesus for who he really is?

Day 3
Matthew 16:13-16

Return in your imagination to the moment between Jesus' significant question, "Who do you say that I am?" and the disciples' answer. Live in the moment of silence, that waiting moment filled with meaning.

Who would have thought it would be impetuous, impulsive Simon Peter who answers the question? Who would have dreamed that the Big Fisherman, uneducated and rough, would be the one who gets it first?

As Jesus, you hear his words of recognition and affirmation, and your heart dances with the joy of being understood. You look into Simon Peter's face and know without a doubt that his confession, his statement of faith, comes from a pure heart. You know by his confession that he is the one who can be counted on to give strength and stability to your mission, even after you are gone.

You smile at Simon Peter. You place your hands on his shoulders and look into his eyes and then give him your blessing and his mission. It is a life-changing moment for Simon Peter. It is the beginning of a whole new chapter in his life. From now on, your lives will be intertwined. Can either one of you possibly know all that lies ahead?

Getting clear about who Jesus is to you will change your life. Have you made that "getting clear" journey?

Day 4

Matthew 17:1-8

What is it about James, John, and Peter that has drawn you to them in an unusual way, Jesus?

You ponder the growing closeness you feel with these three of your disciples as all of you make your way around the countryside. What makes it so easy to talk to them? Do they seem to understand the deeper parts of your teaching more quickly? Is it because their hearts are so open, their spirits so humble?

On this day the four of you are alone, hiking in the mountains. You are free and easy with each other, laughing and talking like old friends. Sometimes you tease each other.

You feel the strain in your calves as you climb higher up into the mountain. You pause to catch your breath. Sometimes Peter goes on ahead; he is strong and agile. The rest of you follow behind him.

As you continue to climb the mountain, you begin to think about some of the mysteries of your life with your father. You wonder how much you should reveal to these friends of your inner circle.

The four of you sit down together in the shade of a tree. You look into each face, and your heart swells with love for these men who have become like brothers to you.

Jesus enjoyed close friendships with men and women. How do you like being friends with him now? How good a friend are you?

65

Day 5
Matthew 17:1-8

Intimately connected to God the Father, Jesus had access to unlimited power and authority. Fully surrendered to the will of the Father, Jesus could transcend normal human limitations and bypass traditional human ways. Fully human and fully divine he was, and while we can identify with his heart and mind to a degree, there comes a point when our finite minds can take us only so far. Nevertheless, we enter into some of the experiences of Jesus and go as far as the Holy Spirit will allow us to go.

What must Jesus have been thinking when he chose to reveal the full splendor of his identity to James, John, and Peter—his friends, his inner circle? Can you imagine that he trusted them enough to let them see the real truth about his identity? Do you think he wanted them to participate with him in the deeper mysteries of his life?

We know, because we walked with him through his temptation experience in the wilderness, that he was not trying to seduce them with sensationalism. Jesus' power was always surrendered to the Father's power, and he never used it for any reason other than to draw others into an intimate, personal love relationship with God.

Think about times when you have "touched the holy" or witnessed Holy Mystery. Why do you think God granted you those times?

Day 6

Matthew 17:1-8

Put yourself back on the mountaintop, right in the middle of the experience Jesus shared with Peter, James, and John.

As Jesus, you are fully aware of the impact this unusual experience is having on your friends. You allow them to see you in your full splendor and, thus, to know more fully who you are. You let them listen in on your conversation with Moses and Elijah, a conversation that illustrates time without boundaries.

You are most fully aware of the power of your father, streaming through your very being. You are acutely aware that all systems are "plugged in"; this is intimacy with the Father in its fullest force.

You are also aware of the reactions of your friends. You see their amazement. You know that they are touched at the deepest level of their hearts and minds by this encounter with the Holy. You know that they are able to recognize that which is holy.

You hear Peter, impulsive Peter, break into your awareness. You hear his request to build a tabernacle and remain on the mountain. You know that they will never forget this moment.

What is your reaction when you witness that which you cannot explain with your logical brain? How do you "take" the Holy?

Day 7

Matthew 17:1-8

Move back to the instance when Peter, James, and John are with you in that holy moment of mystery and grace. You are aware of a bright light enveloping all of you. You know that the light is the presence of the Living God. You also know that the unusual display of power, energy, and presence is solely for the purpose of making you known to your three friends.

Watch your three friends fall down on their faces, fearful and trembling. See yourself stand up and lean down over each one, touching them and speaking words of comfort and assurance.

After such a display of holiness, what do you do? How do the four of you act? All of you must process the experience and its impact on you.

See the four of you standing up. Still, Peter wants to build a memorial and remain on the mountaintop. "Don't we all?" you ask him, smiling and gesturing to the path that will lead you back down the mountain into everyday life. You have been invaded by the Real; real life now beckons.

Hear your voice, instructing the three to keep this experience to themselves. "Some things," you tell them, "are too holy and mysterious to share with just anyone."

From this point on, these three who have special knowledge of your identity will be with you in an unusually close way.

What is the price of being in Jesus' inner circle? The reward?

ONE LAST CHANCE

The Lord's Supper

Matthew 26:20-30

Day 1
Matthew 26:20-30

What was it like for Jesus to participate in the Jewish festivals and observances? As he moved among the people, knowing that his whole life was intended to fulfill the law and to take people beyond the law, how did he feel about the Passover observance, the Feast of Unleavened Bread, and the other holy days in Jewish life?

How did Jesus balance the old and the new in his mind? How much time did he spend comparing the richness of his heritage to the vibrancy of the new way of grace and love? Did he struggle to stand at the meeting place between the past and the future?

Always an observant Jew, Jesus entered into the customs of his day. Picture yourself, as Jesus, gathering with friends to share in the Passover meal, a meal commemorating one of the most significant events in Jewish history.

See yourself walking up the narrow stone stairway to the room where you will share this meal. As you enter the eating area, let your eyes take in every detail of this significant occasion. Look at the table and the way it is arranged. See the candles. Smell the food. Hear the bustling of the servants as they make everything right for the evening. Hear the quiet voices of the disciples. Do they know the significance of this meal with you? Can they possibly know?

What are the most significant observances of your religious tradition?

Day 2
Matthew 26:20-30

Put yourself in Jesus' place, imagining his thoughts and feelings as he shares the Passover meal with his disciples. Imagine yourself talking with your friends. Even as you carry on a discussion with them, you are carrying on an inner struggle and dialogue with your heavenly father.

Feel the growing tension as the inevitable draws near. Look into the faces of your friends and feel the sorrow of knowing that you will leave them soon. Experience the heaviness of the moment as you begin detaching from them in order to follow the will of your father.

You break a piece of bread and share it with John. You pass a goblet of wine to Peter. You motion to a servant, and he brings more olive oil and herbs to your table. You soak your bread in the mixture and savor the tastes that have delighted your senses all of your life. You remember what it was like to share the Passover meal with your family, and your heart lurches.

Look into the face of each man seated with you. Watch their expressions as they talk with each other. Feel the silence of John as he leans against you.

Change is in the air. It is transition time once again. Have you prepared these, your followers, well enough? Have you done enough to show them yourself and your mission? Do they have a clear picture of what it means to be your follower? Do they, these intimate friends, know you?

In transition times how does God help you make the changes?

71

Day 3
Matthew 26:20-30

On this day visualize Jesus at the Passover meal with his disciples gathered around him. Imagine all of the sights and sounds of the evening. Feel the growing intensity within Jesus as he moves into a new level of servanthood and takes on the most intense challenge of his mission. Feel the ache in his heart as he comes to the awareness that things must change and that one of his chosen disciples, Judas, will set the process in motion for the changes.

Put yourself in Jesus' place. How did you decide when to tell the disciples that one them would betray you? Did you debate with yourself about whether to clear the air about that terrible topic? Did you want to spare them from the truth?

Was your heart breaking, Jesus, when you had to face the fact that someone you had chosen to walk alongside you was going to be the instrument of death for you? Did it wrench you to admit that someone with whom you had shared some of your most intimate secrets was about to turn on you? Did you make a mistake choosing Judas? If you had it to do over again, would you still choose Judas to be one of your disciples?

Hear the sound of your voice when you speak the truth about what is to come. Observe the reactions of your friends. See their sadness. Listen to their protests.

When you have to speak the truth, where do you get your strength?

Day 4
Matthew 26:20-30

Enter the scene in today's meditation at the moment when Jesus has spoken the truth about the impending betrayal by one of the disciples. Feel his heartbeat as he speaks up and reveals what is to come. Experience the charge of emotion and then the hush that falls over the room. All eyes are riveted on Jesus. Imagine yourself in that position.

You reach for a loaf of the warm bread. You break it in half, and then you tear off a morsel. See yourself dip the morsel into the bowl of olive oil and herbs. Your eyes, though, continue to meet the gaze of the disciples, one by one.

You extend your hand toward Judas. Your eyes lock with his. Your heart beats more rapidly. You notice that his face flushes and he diverts his eyes, but only for a moment.

Hear your voice as you tell the truth about what you know. See pride and arrogance dance with shame and guilt on his face, and then watch as his features harden. You know that when the curtain goes down on his face, his heart closes also. Your heart breaks, not only for yourself and what you are about to experience, but also for Judas.

"You have a choice," the extended hand proclaims. "You don't have to be the one. You can make another choice."

Judas' eyes shift back and forth. He turns his head ever so slightly, and then he says, "It isn't I."

In what ways does the Judas in you betray the Living Christ?

73

Day 5

Matthew 26:20-30

Begin your meditation today by connecting with the moment when you, as Jesus, offer the morsel to Judas. Feel the power of the moment when Judas recognizes that you know the truth about him and what he is going to do.

Feel the tension grow in the room. The feeling of death is present. The disciples shift, uncomfortable in the presence of that which they do not understand.

As Jesus, you explain things in a terse statement. Then you go on to serve the disciples a meal they will never forget.

As Jesus the teacher, you always use what is near at hand as visual aids. This time you take the bread, bless it, break it, and serve the disciples. You lift the moment to a higher level, however, and speak symbolically of the bread. You say that it is *your body*. Do they remember that you told them you were the bread of life? Do they understand?

You take the wine and thank God for it. Serving each one, you wonder if they remember how you turned the water into wine at the wedding feast. You wonder if they remember that you taught them about new wine bursting old wineskins. Do they understand?

The room grows quiet. You sit in the holy silence with your dearest friends. These are the ones with whom you have lived and laughed. These are the ones you have loved.

God still speaks in symbols. What symbols does God use for you?

Day 6
Matthew 26:20-30

Reenter the scene in the upper room, right after Jesus has served the bread and wine to his disciples. Picture him reclining at the table in silence.

Through his eyes look around the room. Recall other rooms where you have shared a meal with these friends.

Think about the importance of breaking bread with friends. Ponder the fellowship that takes place as you share food. Remember the times all of you have lingered around the table until well in the night, talking about the kingdom of God.

Remember other tables around which you have shared your heart. Think about eating with Mary, Martha, and Lazarus. Remember going to Simon's home for supper. Recall the splendid feast at Zacchaeus' house. How much you have enjoyed living and loving your friends, the ones whom God has given you.

You reach back into your memory and think about the table in Mary's house. Remember how hard she worked to prepare meals that would please and satisfy her family. You can almost taste her special dishes, prepared with love and made more delicious by the tenderness and care with which she did everything.

You sense a finality about things. The nudgings of your father tell you that your time in this world is drawing to an end, and so you gaze with rapt affection at the scene before you. Despite your desires, you know that you must not cling to this moment.

God is present at every ending, bringing birth to new beginnings. When has God helped you let go of what has been precious to you?

Day 7

Matthew 26:20-30

Re-create the scene in the Upper Room. Hear the rustling of the wind outside the window. Watch the servants begin to clear away the dishes. As Jesus, you sense that it is time to go. You know the end is near.

You stand up. Your heart is so heavy, you think you cannot bear the weight of it. Saying goodbye to these friends is almost more than you can bear. How hard it is to let go of good times and close friends! How difficult this separation is for you; how much more it will be for them! They have no idea what is ahead, and neither do you completely.

As if of one heart, you all begin to sing together one of the ancient hymns of your heritage. You listen to the voices blending in harmony and beauty. You want to inhale every sound, every note, every precious word of the blessed music. You feel the presence of your father in the old, old song. What a privilege it is to share a meal and music with your closest friends. You can rely on this moment in the days that lie ahead, drawing strength from the sound of the voices united in song.

See yourself walking steadfastly down the stairs and into the night, the darkest night of your life. Hear footsteps behind you. Your friends follow you to your sacred space.

You walk toward the door. They follow you. You open the door one last time. You don't look back.

Remember your most difficult moment of parting. God was there. What was it like for you to let go of someone you love?

KNOW MY GRACE

As God Incarnate, Jesus walked into peoples' lives and transformed them. He took the raw materials of brokenness and woundedness and made people whole. He forgave sin and freed individuals from the chains of their choices. He gave sight and hearing. We call what he did "grace."

Whenever Jesus met a need, he did it because he loved that person unconditionally and wanted wholeness for him even more than the person wanted it. Jesus did not choose people to heal on the basis of their merit; not one of the persons he changed deserved his mercy. Jesus transformed human beings for one reason—love.

In Jesus we see the human and divine come together in perfect form, in the essence of grace. In Christ we see a picture of God's loving intent toward us. God's intent is always, and in all ways, to draw us into relationship with Him. In every way the Creator of the universe extends grace—unmerited favor—toward us. In Jesus, God showed us exactly what it means to live under and in grace.

Our task, as finite people with limited vision, is to accept the grace of Christ and appropriate it into our lives. As you ponder the meditations that follow, ask for the grace to accept the unconditional favor of our Lord. Ask for the grace to know his pleasure and delight in who you are. Allow the encounters of Jesus to make you more gracious. Then, give his grace to someone else.

CONFRONTATION WITH GRACE
The Samaritan Woman

John 4:1-20

Day 1

John 4:1-20

Today picture yourself coming to terms with the cold, hard facts that your whole life is under scrutiny by the religious establishment. You, as Jesus, know that your heart is right with God's heart. You know that you have the highest good of people in mind. You also know that you are following the guidance of God, your heavenly father.

Yet, whatever you do, the Pharisees are suspicious. No matter how much good you accomplish, your motives are doubted and discussed, interpreted and misinterpreted by people who don't know who you are. To add insult to injury, the Pharisees are making a game of it all by trying to turn you and John into rivals.

As a caring and compassionate human being with an open heart and an open life, you feel the effects of others' doubts and derision. Even though you understand their fears and confusion, you also feel your own frustration at being misunderstood. If only you could connect with the Pharisees' need. If only they recognized their need for the grace and mercy of your father.

Imagine Jesus' making the decision to leave the Judean countryside and go back to Galilee. What did he feel as he walked the dusty road back home? Did he ever question himself?

What do you do when your motives are questioned? How do you handle resistance to your mission in life, your goals, and your work?

Day 2

John 4:1-20

There is the kind of fatigue that comes from expending physical energy, the kind that makes your body ache. There is another kind of fatigue, the fatigue of mental strain, of working too hard or too long to figure out a problem.

Emotional fatigue occurs either when you've experienced strong emotion or when you've had to hold in emotion for too long. Emotional roller coasters, often evoked by the behavior or choices of others, can drain your whole being of creativity and energy.

As Jesus made his way across the countryside and through Samaria, a land that was off-limits for Jews, he grew weary. Perhaps he was tired of trying to get people to do what they didn't want to do, regardless of how good it would have been for them. Likely, he felt the mental strain of meeting intellectual doubts and verbal challenges. He probably felt the emotional strain of dealing with others' resistance and sabotage of his work. Because he was fully human and fully divine, even Jesus felt physical fatigue.

Imagine the fatigue of Jesus as he walked through Samaria. Was it possible that he was so weary, he simply didn't care if he was in "corrupted" areas? Or was he, even as tired as he was, able to see beyond man's restrictions and live above man's taboos so that he could go where he needed to go?

Remember a time when you were bone-weary. Identify with Jesus. What do you want to do when you are emotionally spent?

Day 3

John 4:1-20

On this day use your imagination to create a picture of yourself, as Jesus, sitting at Jacob's well at high noon. Feel the tiredness in your body. Experience the thirst that follows a long, dusty trip. Imagine the sun beating down on your head and the dirt on your feet.

As you rest there, you recall the stories about your ancestors, Jacob and Joseph. You remember the times when Mary and Joseph, your earthly parents, told you about the ways of your forefathers as you sat around the fire at night. From childhood you could picture the stories in your imagination. From your youth you have known that your destiny is a continuation of their story, God's story.

Think about your disciples. Close your eyes. Ponder their reactions to your taking the trip through Samaria. Smile to yourself as you see the expressions on their faces when you decide to stop awhile in Samaria. You still have so much to teach them about following the guidance of God.

As you wait, you feel hunger, the intense hunger that comes when you've been traveling. And you are thirsty, thirsty almost beyond endurance. You look around for something with which to draw water. You close your eyes. You hope the disciples will hurry back.

What was it like to be Jesus, but also to be hungry, thirsty, and tired?

Day 4

John 4:1-20

As Jesus, you are sitting at Jacob's well in Samaria. Suddenly you hear footsteps. When you look up, you see a woman approaching the well. It is high noon. What a strange time to draw water.

You watch the woman. Her head is covered, and she keeps her eyes diverted. Everything about her body language communicates that she wants to be unseen, unrecognized. This is a woman who wants to be left alone. What has hurt her?

Hear your voice as you speak to her. Hear yourself asking her for a drink of water.

How can you do this? You are breaking convention. You, a Jewish man, are not supposed to address a woman in public like this—especially a Samaritan woman.

Do you sense her recoiling from you? Does she wish you would go away? Hear the shock in her voice as she challenges your request. She knows that you, a Jew, aren't supposed to be talking to her.

Do you consider what other people might think about what you are doing? Do you worry about her response? Will she misinterpret your initiative? Or do you, at some deep level of awareness, sense that this is a human being who can understand the deeper mysteries of God? Do you sense her need?

Are you willing to challenge convention for the sake of God?

Day 5
John 4:1-20

Re-create the moment at the well when Jesus initiated a conversation with a woman—a Samaritan woman at that!

Imagine yourself, as Jesus, entering into dialogue with this woman. Watch her carefully. See how she responds. How do you know that you can reach her heart? What is it about her that makes you think you can set her on a different path, a path of freedom, wholeness, and usefulness?

Feel the energy return to your body and mind as you reach out to this woman. Suddenly you aren't thinking about your own fatigue any longer. You aren't focused on your hunger or thirst. You aren't even thinking about the criticism and resistance of the Pharisees you left behind in Judea.

Hear your voice as you question this woman, leading her to confront her own need. You challenge her ideas. You make her think in ways she's never thought before. You give her respect and hope. How does your voice sound as you hold out to her the grace and mercy of your father?

Imagine there is a moment when she dares to raise her eyes to yours and look straight into your face. What do you see in her expression? What stories are written on her face? How do you feel, meeting her heart to heart?

Remember a time when you were able to go beyond your own need to met the need of someone else. What was that experience like for you?

Day 6

John 4:1-20

You are Jesus again today, back at Jacob's well in Samaria. Picture the scene just as you left it yesterday. Hear the song of the birds overhead. Feel the gentle stirring of the wind. Imagine the taste of water in your parched mouth. Experience the excitement of knowing that you are making a connection with another human being in the name of your father.

You tell the Samaritan woman about "living water." She thinks you mean one type of water; you are talking about two distinct realities. You know that she doesn't get it at first. She can only understand ideas from her earthly experiences. She hears from her own perspective. She knows only where she's coming from, not your point of view.

You persevere, however. You make some leaps about her personal life. You challenge her and, in doing so, meet her at the point of her greatest pain. She has given herself—her heart, body, and life—to mortal men. She has let men own and control her, use and abuse her. If she will give her devotion to your father, she will be free. She will experience the living water that satisfies the deepest longings of the human heart. You look in her eyes. You long for her to be whole. Feel the exhilaration when she does understand.

Recall a time when you felt the longing for another human being to know Christ and to experience the living water of his life. How willing are you to risk rejection for the benefit of someone else?

Day 7
John 4:1-20

Pick up the story of the Samaritan woman and the encounter she has with Jesus at the moment when she recognizes the Truth. Imagine what it is like for Jesus to experience that life-changing moment with her.

As Jesus, you watch her come alive. In her excitement she leaves her waterpot at the well and runs toward the village to share the good news of her transformation. How do you feel, watching her run away, knowing that you have made a profound difference in her life?

See yourself, in that moment of deep joy, turn from the well and meet the eyes of your shocked disciples. Experience the change in your own mind and body as you deal with their censure and confusion. Will you let their judgment throw cold water on the moment? How will you deal with their criticism of you?

You walk over to them, reading the expressions on their faces. You reach out to them, smiling. Renewed and refreshed, even without physical sustenance, you begin to tell them about the woman at the well and how she understood who you are.

Watch their faces. Do they understand? Will they accept what you have done? Can they see the big picture of God's purpose in the lives of every human being?

When you are going against convention, can you do it with the conviction and poise of Jesus?

FIRST THINGS FIRST
Jesus and Nicodemus

John 3:1-21

Day 1
John 3:1-21

At the end of the day, where did Jesus go to relax? Did he choose to spend his evenings alone or visit with friends? Who prepared his evening meal? Who ate with him?

After reading today's Scripture text, picture Jesus in a home. Perhaps it is early evening, right after dinner. See the candlelight flickering on a low table. Hear the sounds of servants, putting away the food and cleaning up. Imagine that Jesus is sitting alone, pondering the events of the day. Maybe he is praying, seeking the guidance of God the Father, and listening for that still, small voice he knows so well.

As you imagine yourself in Jesus' place, you hear someone come to the front door and knock. You hear your host go to the door. Someone asks for you. Are you glad to be "found," or do you long for an evening to rest and collect your thoughts? Are you ever too tired to meet one more human need at the end of the day? After all, the hour is late.

You look up and see the religious leader, Nicodemus. You know him by reputation and have seen him at work. He is a Pharisee. You are surprised to see him. What does he want? Has he come as an honest seeker, or is he an adversary? Does he come in peace or to make conflict?

How do you react when you are face to face with someone whom you know is going to question or challenge your faith?

Day 2
John 3:1-21

Return to the moment of encounter between Nicodemus and Jesus. Re-create the room where they met. See the furnishings in the room and the candlelight. Hear the sounds of voices in the background. You can smell the aromas of the evening meal and feel the cool night air, even inside the house.

As Jesus, you wait. You look straight into the eyes of this Pharisee. With your unusual understanding of humankind and your deep sensitivity to the yearnings of the soul, you sense that this man is a true seeker. You admire his courage in seeking you out, even if he did come under the cover of night. You smile slightly and motion for him to sit down.

You notice that Nicodemus begins by calling you "Rabbi." The tone in his voice is respectful. His opening statement reveals that he sees something in you that is different. Nicodemus senses the power that is granted to you by your heavenly father.

You notice that he uses the pronoun "we." He must have been talking this over with other Pharisees. You wonder if he came to find out for himself just who you are and what you are about or if he was sent by the others. You guess that he has come on his own, searching for answers for himself. You know that the answers you have will set him at odds with his group.

How do you discern the motivation of others when they question you?

Day 3
John 3:1-20

Intimately connected with God the Father, Jesus was always ready and able to meet whatever challenges were given to him. Always listening for that still, small voice of guidance from God, he sensed the inner motivations and yearnings of the hearts of the people who questioned him. He could tell the difference between people who wanted to discuss points of religion just to have a good discussion or cause conflict and those whose hearts and minds were open to receive the fresh, new wine of God's grace and love.

Create that scene again as Jesus and Nicodemus dialogue with each other. From what you, as Jesus, know about Nicodemus, you understand that birth and family of origin are of primary importance to him. You are aware that he has gained a great deal in life from being "born well"; much of what he has attained is due to the fact that he was born into a privileged class. When you look into the eyes of Nicodemus, you see a man who is proud of his heritage and has gotten where he is because he was born into the right family.

As Jesus, hear your voice explaining the necessity of "new birth" to Nicodemus. You know, even as you speak, how you are challenging the core of Nicodemus' values.

What difference does being "born well" make today? What difference does it make to you?

Day 4

John 3:1-20

Imagining yourself as Jesus, as you speak with Nicodemus today, you are aware that the idea of talking about the "new birth" to this man is divinely inspired. God has given you the precise imagery and exact words to meet the most basic need of this particular man. You rejoice inwardly at the way you and God work together to complete the task.

As you carry on the inner dialogue with God, gaining guidance and giving thanks, hear the protests of Nicodemus. Aren't they predictable? Isn't he saying exactly what anyone else in his position would say given the challenge you have laid down before him? You have compassion for him; he is thinking as he was trained to think. Nicodemus is thinking on a literal, material plane. Will his mind allow the new wine to enter?

You, on the other hand, are speaking of a far greater reality. You are thinking on a spiritual level that is much grander and broader and more glorious than anything in the material world. How will you get Nicodemus to go beyond his rational thinking? How will you help him make room for the new, bigger reality of the mystery that cannot be measured, contained, or controlled?

You try again. You amplify your first, simple statement. You flesh out the profound truth to make it understandable.

How are you, like Nicodemus, attached to logic and rational thinking?

Day 5
John 3:16

If you had been Jesus, what would you have been feeling as you explained the greatest truth in history to Nicodemus, a respected religious leader? Can you imagine the power of God surging through you as you summed up your whole mission and purpose in this expression of God's love for the whole world?

Hear the passion in your voice as you declare God's generosity and explain God's ultimate intent for humankind. You reach out and grasp the arms of Nicodemus as you speak. Your eyes are ablaze with the vibrant dynamism God has planted in you. With all of your heart you yearn for this man, this leader with influence and worldly power, to understand.

You want Nicodemus to know that the eternal life the Father wants to give through you is not so much about the length of life as the quality of life. It is about living connected with the Father as you are, a connection as intimate as a vine and its branches.

You want Nicodemus to know that this eternal life is available in this moment and that it is a free gift of grace. Keeping laws cannot earn it. There isn't a family positioned well enough to deserve it.

This gift of eternal life is a grace gift, a gift of love. What is it like to want someone else to accept the new birth? What is it like to pour out your heart out in love for someone?

Day 6
John 3:1-20

Put yourself back into the moment of dialogue between Nicodemus and Jesus. Remember what it is like to be engaged in an intense discussion about the things that matter most. Feel your heart beat a little faster. Lose all sense of what is going on around you except the dialogue between the two of you.

Imagine what it is like to confront every belief system on which Nicodemus has depended, used for his benefit, and loved. How does Jesus feel, knowing that he is asking Nicodemus to think in an entirely new way about his relationship with God?

Hear yourself telling Nicodemus that the old ways, based on fulfilling the laws of man, are no longer adequate. Pleasing God by earning points in an elaborate system of works is not the way. In fact, *doing* is giving way to *being*. No longer is relationship to God to be judged by what is on the outside, but how things are on the inside. It is no longer enough to look good. From now on, goodness will emanate from a heart surrendered to the sovereignty of God.

You look at Nicodemus and know that you are asking him to see a new way and to reorder his priorities. Family can no longer be an idol. Position must be dethroned. Keeping rules and laws must be replaced by loving God and each other. Everything must change for Nicodemus from the inside out.

Do you feel comfortable when challenging limited belief systems?

Day 7

John 3:1-20

In that intense moment of invitation into the life of grace, did Jesus know what Nicodemus' response would be? Did he wonder if his words had penetrated through the layers of tradition and custom? Did Jesus know, at some level, what Nicodemus would do with his passionate discourse about God's intent for persons? Did Nicodemus accept the truth of Jesus at that moment, or did he leave and think it over?

Looking back with the benefit of history, it is clear that Jesus' words made an impact on Nicodemus, for he was one of the few who argued for fair treatment of Jesus (John 7:50-52). He also helped Joseph of Arimathea prepare Jesus' body for burial (19:38-42).

In that moment of encounter what was it like for Jesus to have laid his whole heart bare before this man who could either accept or reject Jesus' invitation? What was it like for him to end the discussion, not knowing whether Nicodemus would hold Jesus' truth with respect and honor, or if he would turn on Jesus, using Jesus' words to hurt and destroy him?

Imagine how Jesus must have felt, wanting to connect with this seeker and set him free. Stand with him in the empty room in the moments after Nicodemus left and went home.

When have you poured out your heart for another, longing for God's love to transform them? Who has done that for you?

DOING THE RIGHT THING
Healing the Man with the Shriveled Hand

Mark 3:1-6

Day 1
Mark 3:1-6

Do you know what it is like for people to watch every move you make, evaluating your choices, looking for whatever evidence they need to censure or condemn you? Have you been misunderstood?

As you identify with the actions of Jesus, see yourself as a person at odds with religious leaders who do not understand you. Because they have their traditions to protect and their system to conserve, they follow you everywhere. They watch you closely because you are a threat to them. They are afraid you will confuse the people and shake the foundations of their system.

You walk into the synagogue, the bastion of Jewish legalism. You nod to a friend of your family's. He barely acknowledges you. Quickly his eyes dart around the room to see if anyone else has seen the exchange between the two of you. You notice three of the leaders of the synagogue huddled in a corner whispering to each other. You know that they are talking about you and what you have been doing.

Though you are fully divine and in unbroken conversation with your father, you are also fully human. You feel the sting of suspicion and rejection. You ache when someone turns away from you. You feel the pain of their scorn. But more than all of this, you feel the power of the love of your father and the peace of knowing that you are being obedient to Him and His will for you.

What is it like to be misunderstood? To be watched?

Day 2
Mark 3:1-6

You are Jesus again, standing in the synagogue. Remember the sounds of a group of men talking to each other. Notice the whispers and averted glances of the religious leaders when you walk by them.

Suddenly something important catches your attention: human need. You look through the crowd at a man who has a shriveled hand. You stand still and take in his whole appearance.

You see the man, normal and whole except for the tiny, shriveled hand. You look at each finger, all twisted back upon the palm. It is as if the life-force stopped when it came to his hand. Perhaps an injury stopped the growth process so that the hand could not keep up with the rest of the man's body.

Your heart breaks when the man catches you looking at him. Quickly he pokes his hand into the sleeve of his garment, hiding it from your knowing eyes. He turns around and moves behind a larger man, as if he can hide his shriveled hand from God.

The man's shame about his infirmity hurts you as much as the hand itself. You can see him, as a child, trying to make do with inadequate fingers. You weep when you think about how he must have spent a lifetime trying to compensate for his handicap. What was it like for a little boy to grow up through the difficulties of childhood and early manhood, wanting more than anything to be whole like everyone else?

What does the Great Physician want to heal in you?

Day 3
Mark 3:1-6

As the Son of God, Jesus had the power to heal all illnesses. He met each person at the point of his specific need. Furthermore, each healing served a particular purpose, not only for the life of the one who was healed, but also for those around the person. Always the healing was done to give glory to God.

Visualize yourself as Jesus, standing in the synagogue, with your eyes focused on the man with the withered hand. What makes you choose to heal this man on this day and in this place? What about the others there who also need your healing touch?

You know well that healing this man on the Sabbath will break the Jewish law. You hear the room become deathly still as you walk across the floor, but you are focused on your mission and confident of the Father's impulses as they guide you.

See yourself walk over to the man and stoop down to touch him on the shoulder. He keeps his head ducked, as if in shame, but raises his eyes to look at you and glance around the room.

You increase the pressure of your touch on his shoulder. Hear your voice tell him to stand up in front of everyone. Watch him struggle to rise. See yourself extend a hand to steady him.

Hear the silence of the room fill your ears like thunder. You are aware of eyes piercing your back and of the startled murmuring around the room. As the man stands to face you, however, all but his need and your father's love fade from your awareness.

When did you last risk everything to follow the will of God?

Day 4
Mark 3:1-6

As Jesus, you have walked out on the razor's edge of risk. You have put yourself in a vulnerable position and left yourself open for criticism and censure.

In your imagination see yourself look deep into the eyes of the man with the shriveled hand. Is that fear you see in his eyes, or is it hope? Is he confused and ashamed, or does he sense the power of love emanating from you?

With your strong carpenter's hands, take that lame, shriveled hand in yours and feel every part of its deformity. See yourself cover the top of the man's hand with your other warm, tender hand. Feel the trembling in the man.

Now you turn your head and look around the room. You know what the religious leaders are thinking because you know their law and tradition. You know that what you are about to do is against their law. You are going to be in big trouble.

So you put the question to them. You speak so that everyone in the room hears you. Your words are clear and distinct; your voice is firm and bold. You lay it on the line and force them to think about what really matters.

"Which is lawful on the Sabbath," you ask, "to do good or to do evil, to save life or to kill?"

Your question hangs heavy in the air; the words pierce like flaming swords. You know their impact and the logical, predictable consequences for what you are about to do.

Which is louder for you: the voice of God or the voice of the crowd?

Day 5

Mark 3:1-6

There are moments when you know that you are at a cross-roads, and the decision you make is going to seal your fate, one way or another. Every person looks back on turning points and sees that in a moment, everything changed.

Feel the anger of Jesus as he looks around at the Jewish leaders, religious folks who put their own ideas, rules, and customs ahead of human need. Sense the distress in Jesus' heart as he comes face to face with religious legalism that is more important than the welfare of one of God's children.

Recognize the stubbornness of hearts grown cold with piety and self-righteousness. Feel the stone wall of pride and arrogance. The small hand you hold is withered, but not nearly as withered as the hearts of the religious leaders.

Imagine the moment of freedom that comes when you do the right thing. Feel, with Jesus, the power that comes with living in accordance with the Heavenly Father's loving purpose for one solitary human being. Ponder what it is like to have the boldness of intimate union with the Father.

Feel the gladness as you command the man to stretch out his hand. Look into his eyes. See him look first at you and then at the crowd. You smile at him, encouraging him to dare to be healed. Notice the shift in his face when he connects completely with you and loses his concern with the crowd.

Are you more connected with the Living Christ or with others?

Day 6

Mark 3:1-6

What an incredible experience it must have been for Jesus to heal the sick and restore the lame. How glad it must have made him to hold a withered limb in his hands and feel the power of God's healing force surge through him and into the body of a broken person, restoring life and purpose.

Imagine how it must have been to be God's unhindered and perfect instrument at that moment. What was it like to have been able to cooperate unreservedly with God's healing power?

See in your mind's eye the look on the man's face as the healing force of God Almighty surged through his hand, straightening his fingers and atrophied muscles. Imagine what Jesus must have felt as he watched the look of astonishment and wonder on the face of the man. See the look of gratitude and wonder light up his eyes.

The Great Physician valued one unnamed man and his shriveled hand enough to put his own reputation and life on the line for him. The Prince of Peace loved a cripple in the crowd so much, he was willing to risk everything to give him a new hand. The Son of God was bold enough to stand for love over law and desired freedom for others enough to jeopardize his own.

What are you willing to risk so that others might experience the healing power of Jesus Christ? Your reputation? Your security or comfort? Your logic and reason? Your life?

101

Day 7
Mark 3:1-6

In an instant the murmuring of the crowd begins, first in one part of the room, and then another, building intensity and volume until the room is filled with the sounds of anger and outrage.

If you had been Jesus, having just healed a man on the Sabbath, how would it have felt for you to hear the outrage? Can you hear the individual voices, some louder than others, or do the voices all melt together in one volcanic cacophony?

Feel the people rushing past you; some cringe and draw back into themselves as you walk toward the exit. Humans always find it hard to be in the presence of unconditional love.

People you have known all your life look back over their shoulders at you as they rush out the door. You suppose they are not eager to have it known that they were in the same room when you broke the law. You don't know if they are more frightened or angry, but you do know that underneath all the fury lies fear.

You walk the corridor where people huddle together in tight clusters. Herodians and Pharisees are bonded together in rage. What strange bedfellows politics make!

You walk outside into the clear air. Across the way you see the lame man showing off his hand. You hear him shouting to his friends to come and see what has happened to him. He glances up toward the synagogue and sees you. He points in your direction, and others turn to stare at you. Turning inward to the voice of your father, you know that love is worth the price.

Jesus Christ risked all for you. What difference does that make?

FORGIVING SINS
The Woman Caught in Adultery

John 8:1-11

Day 1

John 8:1-11

Reading the Gospels, it is clear that the key to Jesus' life, work, and ministry was his prayer life. Leaving the crowds behind, he did what he needed to do in order to maintain the constant connection with his heavenly father. Jesus' priority was time spent in communion with God, for that was how he received what he needed to do, what he was commissioned to do. Jesus knew how to find time to be alone so that he could then be with others. He entered the fullness of solitude in order to pour himself out to others.

On this day make your way with Jesus to the Mount of Olives. Walk over the rugged terrain with him to a special place where he can find solace and solitude. Hear the sounds of the night rustling among the trees. Feel the cool night air as you find your favorite place to pray and rest.

As Jesus, you let go of the demands of the day. You release your work into the hands of God, trusting Him with the results. You breathe deeply and still your mind. With the ease of habit and the familiarity of your practice, you open your mind and heart to God, surrendering all of yourself to Him. There in the silence and stillness you focus only on the presence of the Living God.

How high on your priority list is time alone with God?
What are you willing to walk away from in order to be
with God?

Day 2

John 8:1-11

See yourself as Jesus, walking down the Mount of Olives and into the city. Walk through the streets of Jerusalem to the Temple courts. Perhaps you stop and buy a light breakfast.

As you walk through the courts, people call to you and wave. You return their greetings. You savor the morning sounds as people begin the day in their various ways. You love being with people. You enjoy life with others.

A friend joins you as you walk through the courts. He has a burning question. You stop to answer him, giving him your full attention. Soon someone else joins you and interjects another question. Before you know it, a crowd has gathered around you, so you sit down to teach.

Suddenly your informal classroom is interrupted by the sounds of loud voices. You see commotion among the Jewish teachers and Pharisees. They are pushing and shoving each other, yelling accusations at someone in the center of the fracas.

Without warning, one of the most respected leaders emerges from the center of the crowd. He is clenching the arm of a woman. Anger blazes in his eyes. He shoves the woman toward you with such force that she falls to the ground.

You stand up, horrified at the spectacle. Spontaneously, you move toward the woman to help her.

"We caught her in the act of adultery!" the men began to shriek. "She is to be stoned!"

If you were in this drama, which character would you be?

Day 3

John 8:1-11

Take up today's meditation where yesterday's ended. See yourself, as Jesus, standing before the angry mob of Jewish leaders. The woman caught in adultery is at your feet, trembling with fear and shame.

You look into the angry faces. You hear the jeers. Then a white-hot revulsion fills your body; you can taste disgust in your mouth.

You want to ask: "And just how did you know where she was? Which one of you was with her? Why was she caught, but you weren't?"

You hear their demands that you solve their problem. You hear their challenge about Moses' law. You see that this mob fury, left unchallenged, can lead to the stoning of a woman. You know, too, that the one who was with her will go unpunished; the laws protect the strong and powerful, but punish the weak and oppressed. Furthermore, those who accuse her will revel in their self-proclaimed righteousness because they have been tough on adultery. They think that they will have shown themselves to be pure and holy because they have weeded out sin in others.

When you look at these accusers, you see beyond their words and brutal behavior. You see cold, hard hearts. You also see their fear, calloused over by self-righteousness.

Is your heart tender enough to see the real victims in the world?

Day 4

John 8:1-11

Again pick up today's meditation where yesterday's ended. Stand with Jesus in the tense, tight moment of confrontation with the Pharisees and religious teachers. Hear their demand for an explanation. Feel the fury and rage swirling around you. In the pit of your stomach experience the knowledge that what you do and say will shape your fate.

Then look down at the ground at the woman. Notice her torn clothing. See the scrapes on her legs, the bruises on her arm. Watch her as she tries to still her trembling. Observe the way she keeps her head down and her eyes diverted from yours.

You stoop down near her. She flinches, fearful that you will strike, shame, or stone her. She is accustomed to this type of treatment.

You begin writing in the dirt with your finger. The accusers badger you and taunt you, but you are thinking about all of the times when you have seen women used and abused by men. You think about your own mother and what she went through giving birth to you, enduring peoples' gossip and scorn.

Bombarded from without by the mob and from within by your own thoughts and emotions, you continue to write on the ground. As you do, you return, in your own thoughts, to your time with the Father on the Mount of Olives. You reconnect with the power source and detach from the power-brokers. You bide your time and see the Father's guidance.

Are you able to detach from the crowd and connect with God?

Day 5

John 8:1-11

Begin today by picturing how it would have been to be Jesus, stooping down by the woman caught in adultery, writing on the ground. Again hear the challenge of the religious leaders. Which one of *them*, you wonder, was the *man* caught in adultery? Why is it fair that the woman bears the brunt of the sexual sin, you ask yourself? Why is the woman to be stoned, and not the man?

Connected with God the Father, you know what you are to do. You take a deep breath. You feel the power of God well up inside you, replacing the anger you had toward the men and the situation. All you feel now is the love, mercy, and grace of God for all humankind pouring through you. You sense God's approval as you sort through the priorities and put human beings before law. You rise to the occasion of coming to the defense of the oppressed.

"Which one of you is without sin?" you ask, laying the problem back on the shoulders of those who thought they had trapped you. Your voice is strong, but quiet. You are firm, but gentle.

Watch the shock spread on first one face and then another. Notice how their eyes dart back and forth, checking out each others' reactions. One face flushes with the red stain of guilt. Another clenches his fist toward you. Calm and filled with the Holy Spirit, you stoop again and write in the sand.

When have you had the courage to take a stand against evil?

Day 6
John 8:1-11

Connect with Jesus in the moment when he pierces the air with the truth of God. Be with him and feel his heartbeat as he exposes the self-righteousness and dishonesty of those who are filled with their own righteousness and sin.

With his eyes, watch as the accusers begin to skulk away, the oldest one first. The atmosphere is eerily quiet now. All you can hear is the shuffle of their feet.

You look toward the woman lying on the ground. She is looking at you, astonished and amazed. When you meet her eyes, she turns away from you.

Quietly, stooped near her, you ask her, "Where are your accusers now? Does no one condemn you now?"

She can't bring herself to look at you. You notice, however, that she is trembling no longer.

"Stand up," you tell her. You watch her struggle to her feet. Your heart breaks that a child of your father's should be so burdened with shame. You cannot bear it that this one, created in the very image of God, has come to such humiliation. Surely it was for people such as this woman that you have come to do your work.

You look into her eyes. She dares to look at you, though briefly. You smile at her. She doesn't dare to smile. Perhaps, you think, she wonders what you might want from her, like the other men she's known. "I don't condemn you either," you tell her.

What is it like to receive grace and mercy? To give it?

Day 7
John 8:1-11

Replay the intense drama of this passage in your imagination. Freeze-frame the action at the moment when Jesus offers mercy and unconditional love to the woman in the story. Stop everything in that grace-filled instant when he extends hope and wholeness to her.

What would it have been like to have pronounced forgiveness for this woman, knowing that it was coming from God, through you, to her? How would it have felt to have had Christ's heart of compassion toward that specific woman in that precise event?

Hear yourself challenging the woman to live a new way. Hear yourself telling her that she has to stop what she has been doing and start new behaviors. You want her to know that for forgiveness to be appropriated, radical change must take place.

You watch the woman walk away. You notice that she stands a little straighter and walks with a little more pride and confidence. You wonder what she will do. Will there be friends to support her new life? Should you follow her and make sure she understands the terms of her freedom? Will she be protected from those who might try to entrap her in the old ways? Will the system she is in even allow her to change? As she walks away, you pour out your blessings to her.

Do your actions help God appropriate mercy and grace?

FACING PERSISTENCE
The Canaanite Woman

Matthew 15:21-28

Day 1

Matthew 15:21-28

Jesus is on another trip, moving around the countryside and encountering one challenge after another. What is it like for him to be on the move all the time? How does he feel about being unsettled? Does he ever long for the comforts of his own home? Does he miss his family?

On this first day picture him at a home with friends. He and his disciples have just arrived at the home of an acquaintance. Before they get settled in this place, a Canaanite woman who lives in the hills appears at the front door.

As Jesus, you hear the sounds of the woman's voice. You can tell that she is determined to see you. You hear anxiety in her voice, but you also hear a certain firmness. This is a woman on a mission, and she will not be deterred by your host who is trying to protect you.

See yourself going on about your business. You hang up your outergarments. You get a drink of water. You may even stretch out on the bed to rest. Even you must take time to rest, especially when you have given so much to other people. You doze off, but you can still hear the woman arguing with your host. How do you respond to the woman's persistent voice?

How do you respond to an irritating problem that just won't leave? How do you deal with that problem?

Day 2
Matthew 15:21-28

Start today's meditation by recalling the scene in Tyre and Sidon in which Jesus visits the home of an acquaintance.

Envision yourself as Jesus, trying to rest. Look around the room, a room that is strange to you. Take in every detail of the walls, the window, and the furniture. Smell the dinner cooking. Feel the rough texture of the blanket on the bed. Take a cool drink of water and then close your eyes and try to rest.

Still, the woman at the front door persists in seeing you. Her voice, firm and strong, permeates the house. You hear first one, and then another, of the disciples try to deal with her. At first they tell her you aren't available. Then they try to convince her to come back at a later time. Finally you hear their exasperation as she refuses to leave.

One of the disciples knocks quietly on the doorframe of your room. You tell him to come in.

"She won't go away," your friend tells you. "She is determined to see you. What shall we do? She's driving us crazy."

You sigh and sit up. You rub your eyes. Even now you can hear her voice, quietly explaining to your host that she must see you.

You rub your neck and rotate your shoulders. How strange it is, you tell yourself, that a *woman* has such audacity with men! How unusual it is for a *Canaanite* woman to be so bold with a Jew!

What reason might you use to keep yourself away from Jesus?

113

Day 3
Matthew 15:21-28

As Jesus, you begin today's meditation by picturing yourself walking out of the privacy of your room and into the main room of the house where you are staying. Your host is standing at the door, trying to block the woman's entrance.

You pause and look at the woman. She begins to pour out her story to you. You ignore her and walk into the eating area and sit down at the low table where the evening meal is to be served.

Is this Jesus ignoring human need? Is it possible the Savior is not paying attention to a crisis that has come to his front door and demanded attention?

What is going on in Jesus' mind when he ignores this woman and her desperate situation? What is the state of his heart? How can he look into the face of need of this kind and then walk away?

The disciples follow you into the eating area, complaining to him about the woman. You listen to them, and then you dismiss her problem. You tell them that you have enough to take care of with the lost sheep of Israel, your own people. You have your hands full with the Jews and all the needs of your own kindred.

Look at the faces of the disciples, Jesus, when you make what seems to be a heartless and cold response. How do they respond to your indifference to this woman and her great need? How do you explain to them where you draw the line of mercy?

Has there been a time in your life when you felt ignored by God?

Day 4

Role-play Jesus' ignoring of the Canaanite woman. What expression does he have on his face? How does he look when he explains his position to the disciples? Return to the meditation in the moment of Jesus' denial of the woman's request.

As Jesus, you begin to eat. You pick up a loaf of bread, break it, and dip it in olive oil and herbs. The crumbs from the bread scatter on the table and fall to the floor. You lift a goblet of wine to your mouth.

You cannot believe your eyes or ears. The woman has broken all rules of decorum. Even you are astounded at her brashness. Or is she so desperate that her need has distorted her thinking processes? Perhaps her need is so great, she no longer cares about rules.

You watch as the woman makes her way straight to you. You notice the anxiety written across her face, a face that shows the wear of sleepless nights and agonizing days.

See the woman fall down on her knees in front of you. Look at her rough, calloused hands as she clasps them in desperate petition before you. Hear her plead with you, "Master, help me."

You go into the inner kingdom and seek guidance from your father. You thought that you were sent for the children of Israel. What does God say to you?

Is there a part of you, one of your "many selves," that is desperate for the healing touch of the Master?

Day 5

Matthew 15:21-28

Let your imagination create the sights and sounds of this remarkable encounter between Jesus and a person with three strikes against her. She is a woman, a Canaanite, and has broken all the rules of the culture by flinging herself at the feet of Jesus. If you were Jesus, what would you do?

You are aware of the shocked faces of the disciples whom the woman has worn down in her insistence on seeing you. You sense the embarrassment of your host who cannot protect you from her. Within the recesses of your heart, however, you sense the still, small voice of God, a voice growing stronger the longer you follow Him.

You look through a window and see little dogs leaping around the children who are playing in the courtyard. One of them, a young boy, is eating a slice of bread. A playful puppy leaps around him, licking up the crumbs that fall to the ground.

"I can't take bread out of the children's mouths and give it to the dogs," you tell her, thinking she will get your point. Your message is for the children of Israel, and you mustn't give it to the wrong people.

As soon as the words are out of your mouth, the woman comes back at you with a quick and reasonable retort of reason. Even more significant is the tug God makes on your heart, a tug that shows you the way of true servanthood.

Do you have one particular problem you have not been able to solve even with all of your own strength and ability?

Day 6

Matthew 15:21-28

Take a moment to open your mind and heart to the presence of the Living God. Ask God to reveal to you how it must have felt to be Jesus, there in the room with the Canaanite woman and her bold persistence.

As Jesus, look into her eyes. See the desperation. See the lines of worry etched around her eyes that appear too old for her years.

But when you look at her with the heart of God instructing you, you see something more than her weariness and terror. You go beyond the external problem and see her absolute trust in you. Are you surprised to see trust in the eyes of a Canaanite?

You become fully aware that the room is so still, you could hear a pin drop. It is as if all of the disciples are holding a collective breath, waiting to see how you will respond to this woman. Time stands still. You know this is a test for you, a test allowed by God your father. How you respond to this woman will make a difference in her life and also yours.

How often have you seen that depth of faith in the eyes of one of your own people? When have you seen that kind of trust and belief in you from one of the religious leaders of your own race? Do your own disciples look at you with that degree of single-minded devotion? What will you do, Jesus?

If you don't get the answer you want, do you persist with Jesus?

Day 7

Matthew 15:21-28

As if you were an artist, paint the scene in this Scripture on the canvas of your mind. See the characters. Hear the sounds. Smell the aromas of food cooking.

Picture Jesus squaring off with a woman in need. Look at his body language, facial expressions, and gestures. Imagine you can feel his heart and what he is experiencing as he begins to open his own mind and heart to a broader mission field than the Jews. Instructed by the indwelling presence of God's spirit, Jesus is led through his mission day by day.

Now imagine you are in Jesus' shoes. Suddenly everything in you shifts. You sense at the deepest level of your being the faith in this woman. You know that you cannot *not* respond to her. You can do no other than to grant her request. This is a woman whose purity of heart matches few people you have encountered, and you are not going to let her down.

Hear the joy in your voice as you grant her deepest desire. With your unusual powers of healing and your God-breathed abilities, you pronounce the daughter well.

Look at the woman's face when she knows the truth. See her ecstasy. Notice the gratitude in her eyes. Know that you have done your father's will.

Can you allow the Living Christ in you to give grace to the unacceptable part of yourself?

LIFTING PEOPLE UP
Zacchaeus

Luke 19:1-10

Day 1
Luke 19:1-10

Imagine yourself as Jesus, walking around the town of Jericho. See yourself stopping at the fruit stalls and buying a succulent piece of fruit. Pause to speak with an old man. Exchange greetings with the vendors. Take time to share a joke with a friend.

You love being with people. You enjoy the venture of seeing what people will cross your path within a given day. You rise to the challenges they make to your teaching. You savor the opportunity to make a difference in someone's life.

As you walk along, you think about the people you've healed and wonder how they are doing. You remember those who have listened to you, some with open hearts and others with questioning minds. You wonder how they are doing, appropriating the truth that will set them free.

You remember your mission statement. You say it to yourself, quoting form the Holy Scriptures. You know more and more that your reason for being is to set people free, to open blind eyes, and to proclaim the day of the Lord. This day, every day, is "the day of the Lord," the day to experience the presence of the Living Lord.

Who will cross your path today? Who needs you today? What prisoner will come to you with chains that need to be broken? What will be asked of you on this, the Lord's day?

As you start your day, do you open your mind and heart to God?

Day 2

Luke 19:1-10

You are Jesus, walking along the streets of Jericho. A single cloud drifts across the clear, blue sky. You hear the song of a bird in a nearby tree.

Taste the fruit you have bought. Hear the sound of children laughing. Hear the gurgle of a fountain in the square. Feel the warm sun on your body. Raise your face to the sky in sheer gladness at being alive and about your father's business.

As you walk through the village, people join you. You banter easily with them. You really like being with people; you enjoy the dynamics of interaction with other men and women. You love children and your friends.

You are fully present when you communicate with people. You hear what each one says. You understand not only with your mind, but also with your heart. You take every question seriously. Never do your eyes dart around, looking for someone more interesting.

At the same time that you are aware of the specific person with whom you are engaged in conversation, you also notice, at another level of awareness, what is going on around you.

Ahead of you, then, you notice the strangest thing. You look more closely. Is that a man in the sycamore tree? Can it be? Is that really a man and not a child? He has on the clothes of a businessman. You look more closely and recognize the man. It's Zacchaeus, the tax collector.

God often shows up in unusual situations and "different" people. Are you watching? Will you recognize Him?

Day 3
Luke 19:1-10

Imagine how it is for Jesus to walk along the streets of Jericho and enjoy the day. Experience with him the surprise of spying a grown man perched in a sycamore tree.

Imagine what it is like to live with a mind and heart open enough to delight in the unexpected surprises, the out-of-the-ordinary encounters, and the sometimes strange and unusual situations into which he is led. With his heart, feel how it is to be available to those interruptions of ministry.

Imagine what Jesus thinks and feels when he sees Zacchaeus in the sycamore tree. What is his reaction? Does he want to laugh? Does he want to ask, "What on earth are you doing up in that tree?" Does he want to make some kind of comment about the inappropriateness of a businessman being up in a tree in the middle of the day?

Or does Jesus' heart instruct him, making him aware of the sensitive nature of this moment? Does the compassionate heart of Jesus, informed always by the loving voice of God the Father, make him sensitive to the risk Zacchaeus has taken? Jesus would never embarrass anyone, especially an honest seeker.

Picture the moment of encounter. Feel the connection when your eyes meet Zacchaeus' eyes. Understand Zacchaeus' heart, even if you do think his behavior is a little strange.

What are you willing to risk to encounter the Living Christ?

Day 4
Luke 19:1-10

Pick up today's meditation at the moment when Jesus locks eyes with Zacchaeus. As Jesus, hear the murmurings in the crowd. You think you hear a twitter, too. You have to admit that it is rather amusing to see Zacchaeus perched in the tree.

Hear your voice when you tell him to come down from the tree. You surprise yourself, perhaps, when you tell him that you are going to his house. Even you, Jesus, usually wait for an introduction into peoples' homes and hearts, don't you?

Notice that Zacchaeus has absolutely no embarrassment. On his face is written pure delight.

You watch him scramble down from the tree, holding out a hand to steady him as he jumps to the ground. Standing tall as you are, you realize how short he is and realize that he had climbed into the tree not to hide, but to see you from a better vantage point. Your heart goes out to him.

When you look into the eyes of this man, you see way down deep into his soul. With the inner guidance of God the Father, you perceive his longing and his need. You know that he is tired of the way he has been living. He has come to the end of his rope. He must have gotten to the place of knowing his own need, or he wouldn't have gone to such lengths to see you. You always have compassion for honest seekers, don't you?

Is there someone outside your circle who is searching for Jesus?

Day 5
Luke 19:1-10

Put yourself in Jesus' shoes again. Ask the Holy Spirit to help you see with his eyes and hear with his ears. Ask for the mind of Christ. Most important, ask for the heart of Christ. Know his longing for the wholeness and freedom of every human being.

Reconnect with Zacchaeus in your mind's eye. Stand there on the streets of Jericho with Zacchaeus and notice the delight in his face. He is thrilled that you are going home with him. What an honor for him! He had never dreamed he would be so fortunate. He was hoping only for a glimpse of you as you walked along the streets with other, more deserving people.

You can't keep from getting caught up in Zacchaeus' excitement. You, too, are overjoyed, but . . . wait. What is that murmuring around you?

Everyone is grumbling and complaining. Like a bunch of spoiled children, they pout about your taking up with Zacchaeus. Why, they are even questioning your motives as if they are better than Zacchaeus.

Turn and look into the faces of each person. Hear the quibbling subside as you look deep into their eyes, one by one. Notice how they cannot sustain eye contact with you; they look to the ground, ashamed of themselves.

You hear Zacchaeus begin to apologize. Your heart breaks for him, but it breaks more for closed hearts.

Does the quibbling of others divert you from your mission?

Day 6

Luke 19:1-10

Imagine yourself as Jesus, standing in the middle of a crowd of people. You hear their complaints about the fact that you are choosing to go home with Zacchaeus. You also hear Zacchaeus' apologies.

Connected to the heart of God, you listen. You turn within to seek the guidance of your father. You want to know His perspective on this situation. You know that He sees to the heart of each one. Your heart breaks when you realize how often human beings judge each other only by what they see on the outside.

Empowered by the presence of your heavenly father and informed by Him, you speak up so that everyone on the streets can hear you. Confident that you are doing the right thing and even more confident that you are doing the loving thing, you turn toward Zacchaeus and tell him the good news about his life. You announce to him that salvation has come to his house, and you position him within the inheritance of grace.

You put your hand on Zacchaeus' shoulder. The two of you begin to walk toward his home, talking as if you are old friends. You are aware that those you leave behind may or may not understand. You do know they will talk about you—you hope they will.

Is there an unacceptable part of you with whom Jesus would like to get acquainted? Will the acceptable parts of you let him?

Day 7

Luke 19:1-10

Use your imagination to picture yourself as Jesus leaving Zacchaeus' house. You have enjoyed a meal at his table, received his hospitality, and met his family.

As you walk down the streets of Jericho toward your own resting place for the night, relive the day's happenings. When you started out your day, you had no idea what the turn of events might be. Little did you know that you would find your day's task in a tree.

Hear the questions Zacchaeus asked you as you sat at table. Remember the longing in his eyes as he asked you if this new life you offered could possibly be for someone like him. Recall the tears that streamed down his face as he recounted the stories of his life. Weep as you recall how he told you the many ways he had tried to set his own life right, to pay for his sins, and to atone for his abuses.

You have been an instrument of grace and mercy once again, Jesus. You have set another prisoner free. You have opened blind eyes and set a household on a different path—a path of hope and joy, faith and peace, grace and mercy.

You look toward the heavens and turn within. You give thanks to your father for sending you on such a fulfilling mission. You give thanks for the opportunity to work hand in hand with him. You pray that all you said and did in Zacchaeus' presence will connect him forever to the Father.

What is it like, knowing that you are partnering with God?

KNOW MY POWER

How does God, who is all-powerful, appropriate His power? To understand God better, look at the ways Jesus used power. How would the Creator of the universe, who is omniscient and omnipresent, accommodate Himself to peoples' needs and still maintain His sovereignty? How would God reconcile His power with His love?

What did Jesus, who was God, do with this ultimate power? Did he have to grapple with decisions regarding the expression of his might? Did Jesus use the resources granted to him to meet human needs even as he carried out the instructions of his heavenly father? How did all of that work when Jesus was in human form?

Did Jesus ever withhold power completely? Did he ever struggle with the misuse and abuse of power? What did he do when persons in high positions wielded power over him? Did he ever hold back or restrain himself? Did he ever use his power to make a point? How did he point people beyond himself and toward God the Father?

Imagine what it was like for Jesus, the omnipotent one, to put on human limitations in order to identify with people. Try to put yourself in Jesus' shoes as he responded to those who did not understand his power. Think about what it was like for others to question and challenge him. What was it like for Jesus when others wanted him to use his power for their own self-centered purposes?

MULTIPLYING
LOAVES AND FISHES
Feeding the Hungry

John 6:1-15

Day 1

John 6:1-15

On this day imagine yourself walking with Jesus to the far shore of the Sea of Galilee, away from the throngs of people who are following him.

Perhaps he is trying to get some space and time alone. Maybe he wants to spend some quality time with the disciples, away from the curiosity-seekers. He needs to explain things to the disciples, hear their questions, and respond to their concerns about what they are seeing and hearing.

Imagine yourself as Jesus walking up the gently sloping mountainside, overlooking the lake. Hear the voices of the disciples, bantering with each other. Feel the loveliness of the day, the beauty of your father's world. Look overhead and see the clear blue sky. Savor the moment as you walk away from the demands of the crowd.

You find a resting place and sit down on the ground. One by one your disciples sit down around you. You enjoy them so much. They are such good company; how much you treasure time spent with them. You look into each beloved face and give thanks to the Father for leading you into a deeper relationship with these than you have with the masses. You wonder where your conversation will take you today.

Do you want to be part of the crowd or Jesus' friend? Are you a curiosity-seeker or a disciple?

Day 2
John 6:1-15

Using the God-given gift of imagination, return to the scene on the hillside, overlooking the Sea of Galilee. Picture yourself, as Jesus, relaxing with the disciples.

As you enter into his experience, you watch the expressions on the faces of each person. Ever sensitive, you notice when you really connect, heart to heart. You also observe when one of them stumbles over some truth you want the disciples to understand. You are infinitely patient with their questions. You want them to question as far as their intellects will allow them, for you want them to be certain of what they are learning from you.

You feel their excitement in the truth that will set them free. You sense their eagerness about the task you share. You also are keenly aware that they have given up much to follow you. You don't take their devotion to you lightly. In fact, you ponder much the cost of discipleship.

Suddenly you notice the crowds coming toward you. How do you react? Do you deal with interruptions with aplomb and equanimity, trusting the Father's timing in all things? Do you ever get just a bit irritated when your task goes uncompleted or your current purpose is thwarted?

Your awareness, connected always to the Father's, informs you that these are hungry people. You are deeply moved that they are seeking you out in spite of their physical hunger.

How do you balance the needs of your family with the needs of others?

Day 3

John 6:1-15

Put yourself in the shoes of Jesus as you pick up the meditation on the scene on the hillside. Hear the noise of the crowd as they seek out time with you. Notice the expressions on the faces of the disciples as they realize their quiet time with you, their teacher and friend, will be interrupted one more time. How will you balance the needs of the crowd with the needs of these whom you have chosen to work with you? What about your needs, Jesus? Do you get hungry, too?

As soon as you notice the physical hunger of the crowd, you are guided to the solution for their hunger by the indwelling spirit of your father. You know what you are going to do and how you are going to do it, but you also seize the moment to illustrate something magnificent for the disciples. You know that you will meet the physical needs of the crowd, but what you are about to do is really for the disciples' benefit.

You ask Philip how you will feed the crowd. You are pretty sure it hasn't occurred to him to think it is his responsibility. The disciples think the crowd should have brought their own lunches. In fact, some of them are ready to send the crowd away.

Andrew points out that a small boy has a simple lunch of loaves and fishes. Is he being sarcastic? Does he think the small picnic might meet your need, Jesus?

What is the greatest inadequacy in your own life right now?

Day 4

John 6:1-15

Entering into the hillside drama, put yourself once again in Jesus' place. Hear the crowd, hungry and needy. Feel their deeper hunger of the soul. Notice the expressions on the faces of the disciples. Feel their confusion. Walk with the disciples up to the very edge of their faith in you and then feel yourself ready to push them over the edge into deeper belief, faith, and trust.

As Jesus, you hear their words. They think there is no way to feed the crowd of people. It is such an improbable assignment and an impossible task, they don't even take you seriously when you beckon to the small boy to bring you his lunch. They are so focused on the insignificance of the boy's lunch, they don't know that the young boy's food is all you need.

Stand there, Jesus, in the midst of the crowd. Move more deeply into the inner sanctuary where you and the Father are one—one mind, one heart, one will. Listen carefully for the still, small voice of His guidance. Feel His pleasure in who you are. Relish His joy in giving Himself and the full range of His power and energy to you to be used in the service of others. Connect with the Father, Jesus, as if you were connecting to the ultimate power source.

When you are faced with the impossible, or when you realize your own inadequacies, what do you do?

Day 5

John 6:1-15

On this day align your heart with the heart of Jesus as he turns his attention to the small boy who has the lunch of loaves and fishes.

Stand there and look at the child. Notice his eyes, gazing up at you in amazement. Does he wonder why you want his lunch? Does he give it to you eagerly, or is he reluctant, wondering what he is going to do to quiet his hunger pangs?

Notice his hair and clothes. Look around to see if his mother or father is nearby. Ask him his name. Stoop to hear it, and then put your hand on his head, blessing him.

You look at his lunch, smiling at the five small barley loaves. You are pretty sure his mother baked those. You look at the two small fish. Likely, his father provided those for him. You hope he will understand, for just a moment, and let you have them.

You look around the crowd and then tell the disciples to have everyone sit down. Hear the hush fall over the crowd. Does everyone sense that they are in the presence of mystery and miracle? Does everyone understand that this is a holy moment when the divine invades the ordinary in an extra-ordinary way? You raise the food to the Father and give thanks. And then, miracle of miracles, there is enough food for everyone.

What insignificant thing do you hold in your hands? What would happen if you placed that resource in the hands of God?

Day 6
John 6:1-15

Re-create in your mind's eye the entire scene of this passage. See the crowd. Watch the disciples. Experience the magnificence of the moment when the humble picnic lunch of a young boy becomes the means for feeding an enormous crowd.

We can go only so far in imagining what it is like to be Jesus. We cannot walk over the boundary between the human and the Divine. Always the holiness of God stops us where He wants us to stop, and we must stand in awe and reverence at the power of Almighty God.

As much as you are able, however, imagine the power of God coursing through you so that you are able to meet the needs of humankind in a specific way and in such abundance that there is leftover blessing. Feel the thrill of knowing you are in perfect attainment with the Living God.

As you walk through the crowd, you enjoy satisfying the physical hunger of these people. Even more, though, you long for every human being to know that you are the Bread of Life, the only source that fully satisfies the deepest longings of the human soul. How will you communicate your adequacy for their needs? How will you make sure that they know you are able to meet them at the point of their every need? How will you show the extent of your love for them?

With what do you try to fill the God-shaped vacuum in your heart? How do you try to satisfy the hunger of your soul?

Day 7

John 6:1-15

Today imagine what it would be like to be in the shoes of Jesus. You have demonstrated your power in a magnificent way. The crowd has left. Your disciples have picked up enough leftovers to fill twelve baskets. Reenter the scene as the day is drawing to a close.

You listen to the talk of a few stragglers who are watching you. Here and there one of the disciples is trying to explain what you have done to a person whose physical need has been met.

Suddenly you begin to hear words that set your teeth on edge. "He must be our king," one says. "We'll crown him ourselves!" another declares. "This is the beginning of a new rule." You know there are many who have not understood.

Always alert to being misunderstood, you know that you must retreat to spend time with your father, so you send the disciples away and turn in the direction of the mountain you love so much.

You seek solitude, not to escape so much as to reconnect with your father. It is not that you would shun community or intimacy; rather, you must give priority to the time of receiving from God. It is only by staying in unbroken communion with the Father that you will stay focused on your mission and how you are to do it.

Are you sensitive enough to God that you know when it is time to draw away into solitude and communion with Him?

ORDER OUT OF CHAOS

Healing the Demon-Possessed Man

Mark 5:1-20

Day 1
Mark 5:1-20

Take some time to be still and rest in the quietness of the moment. Ask the Living Christ to inspire your imagination and guide your thoughts. Ask God to open your mind and heart to receive the gift He has for you today.

As you move into the scene in this series of meditations, imagine the sights and sounds of the event. See Jesus step out of the boat. Watch his disciples climb out of the boat and join him by the edge of the sea. Hear the water lapping against the shore. Smell the early morning freshness of the day.

On the hillside, within sight of the lake, is a cemetery. From the cemetery walks a man known as "the mad man." The man's reputation is well known. You know how much disturbance he creates wherever he goes. In fact, he is such a problem that the only place he can reside is among the tombs.

Put yourself in this scene as Jesus. Watch the man coming toward you. What do you expect from him? What will he say to you? Will he be hostile toward you? Will he create a disturbance that will defeat your work? Is he a danger to himself or to any of your disciples?

You turn inward, as always, and seek the guidance of your father. He has sustained you through the dramatic events of the past few hours; He's there for you now.

Is seeking God your immediate response to trouble? If not, why not?

Day 2
Mark 5:1-20

Take all the time you need to paint a visual image of Jesus'
encounter with the demoniac, the "mad man." With all your
physical senses, enter into the picture.

As Jesus, you stand face to face with a human being whose
condition falls far short of your father's intent for him. With
the heart of Jesus, feel the deep sorrow over one of God's children being bedeviled by forces that have him in such a state of
despair.

With the keen powers of observation Jesus has, you take it
all in. You smell the stench of the unwashed, filthy man. You
notice every sore on his ravaged body, every rent in his clothing, and every smear of dirt on his skin. You are repelled by
the matted hair and the grotesque contortions of his face. You
feel the force of the negative energy that has a grasp on him.

You hear the voice, which was intended to praise God,
erupt in dissonance and incoherence. You notice hands, which
were made to embrace, flail about. Eyes that were meant to
sparkle with joy dart wildly from face to face. Your heart
breaks.

As Jesus, you also move beyond your own repulsion and
see beneath this outer layer to a man tortured by pain and
anguish. You look beyond his behavior and know his shame
and guilt. You sense his rage and hatred. You feel his fear.
Something terrible is in control of this man, and you know
what it is.

*Imagine Jesus looking at your own brokenness. How is it
for him? How is it for you to be seen by the Savior?*

Day 3
Mark 5:1-20

With the compassion of Jesus, you move into the moment when you stand with the "mad man." It is hard, but you let yourself smell, see, and hear all there is about this man.

With your keen understanding, you take it all in. You think about what it has meant for him to have so much anguish within him that he has nearly destroyed himself. You think about what it has been like for him when others have tried to restrain him, doing the only thing they knew to do. You understand that people are frightened by him and that when people are afraid, they try to control what is scaring them.

You ponder how every person is made to live in relationship with other human beings. You think about how hard it has been for this man, created in the image of your father, to live in isolation among the tombs. What has it been like for him, out there alone at night with his demons of fear, shame, guilt, anger, hate, and inferiority? You shudder when you think of all the ways those particular demons keep people imprisoned in alienation and isolation.

Is there a spark left within this man, you wonder? Is there an aspect of him that is sane? Is there some part of his mind, heart, and will that has not been taken over by the demons? Is there any way to restore him to a condition consistent with God's intent for him?

What are your demons? How do they distort God's intent for your life and work? How do they keep you isolated from others?

140

Day 4

Mark 5:1-20

Use your imagination to picture Jesus and the "mad man." Notice the expressions on the disciples' faces. See stragglers from the hillside come close, curious about how you will handle one of their outcasts, a monster who has been a constant problem for them and a disruption to their tranquillity.

As Jesus, connected intimately with the power of God, you hear your voice command the evil spirits to come out of the man.

You watch the man come up to you and bow and, almost at the same moment, resist the healing power of your father. You are painfully aware of how hard it is for evil to let go of a human spirit. You know that the closer a person gets to you, the more evil fights to stay in power. You stand your ground, however, for the voice of your father reminds you that His power is always greater than the power of the evil one.

"What is your name?" you ask the man, grounding him in the most basic of all knowing. You know what his name is, but you want to know if he knows.

"My name is Legion," he says. You know that he speaks the truth. Indeed, he is many persons in one—split, torn, and fragmented. He is a man at war with himself, struggling against himself in all ways. This is a man who is out of harmony, disconnected, disoriented, and confused. This is a man in the grips of evil itself.

How well do you know your many selves? Can you tell when evil has the upper hand with you? What name do you call yourself?

Day 5

Mark 5:1-20

Again we can only go so far, walking in Jesus' shoes. We can walk right up to the point where the human Jesus and the divine Jesus meet, but we cannot cross over. Our imaginings can take us only a limited distance.

On this day, however, the challenge is to get in touch with the intent of Jesus for the "mad man." Imagine Jesus, in perfect harmony with his heavenly father, seeking His guidance and power. Imagine how God the Father gave Jesus what he needed to give harmony to this broken, fragmented man.

Picture the moment when Jesus looked into the face of this disowned creature. What was it like for him to be able to take command over the demons that were splitting this man asunder and to speak the words that would cast them out? What did it do to Jesus to watch peace and serenity settle over the man's countenance. After speaking the words that cast out the demons of fear, shame, guilt, hate, anger, and inferiority, how was it for Jesus to observe the transformation that occurred in this precious person?

Stand with Jesus and observe order descending within the man's inner being. Feel the gladness in your heart as healing, restoring, transforming love emanates from you to him. Watch the demons let go. What is it like for you? At the same moment hear the hush of the crowd and the clamor of the crazed pigs, stampeding down into the lake.

Imagine Jesus transforming your fears and making you whole. In what ways does he want to use you to bring order and harmony in your world?

Day 6
Mark 5:1-20

Stand with Jesus in the moment when the demons leave the man and enter the pigs. Watch chaos disrupt the pastoral tranquillity of the grassy hillside. Notice what happens when everything falls apart.

With the eyes of Jesus, picture the scene as the pigs, crazed and out of control, race down the hill and into the water, drowning themselves within a matter of minutes.

See the people who were tending the pigs chase them. Hear the terror in their voices. Responsible for the welfare of the animals and accountable to the owners, they panic. You know that they are fearful for their own safety and economic security, and are scared that the demons might enter them.

It is so much easier for evil to be located in one man. How simple things are when there is a scapegoat in a town, one person upon whom all the blame can be laid. What a problem it is for the whole town when everyone must get into the fray. How complicated it is when one person's healing and transformation disturb the whole system.

As Jesus, you see the expressions of terror in their faces as they come to you to find out what is happening. At first they are in awe of you, and then the anger takes over again. You see that underneath all the rage and fury is fear. You know that it is not your father's will for any of His children to live in fear.

God heals systems by healing persons. Where is God at work today?

143

Day 7

Mark 5:1-20

How does the healing of one person cause trouble for others? Doesn't Jesus realize that casting out the demons in one man will be hard on the economic system of others? And what about those animals? How like Jesus to put humans above any other part of creation—love over law!

Imagine the intensity Jesus must have felt in this dramatic story. From the perspective of Jesus, see the townspeople, wanting to discover what has happened and to observe the mad man wearing decent clothes and talking coherently. Feel the surge of energy in the air as the people try to process the events. Let yourself experience the crosscurrents of opposing need as the old dies and the new is born.

Hear the people tell Jesus to leave. How does Jesus feel? How is it for Jesus, knowing that the very ones who want to banish him also have demons of fear, guilt, shame, hate, anger, and inferiority that limit and cripple them? How is it for him to realize that these who are casting him out of their neighborhood also need to be set free by him?

Hear Jesus tell the man to go home to his own people and share his story. What causes him to do this? What does Jesus feel, knowing that one man's healing has changed the dynamics of the whole system in which he lives?

How has your own spiritual growth caused difficulty for the systems in which you live? Does your family system support the health of all its people? What about your family of faith?

THE WRATH OF GOD
Cleansing the Temple

John 2:12-25

Day 1

John 2:12-25

What is it like for you after a big event? When was the last time you gathered with family and friends to mull over a major happening all of you shared?

Picture Jesus in Capernaum with his mother, brothers, and disciples in the days after he performed his first miracle, the changing of the water into wine at the wedding feast. Put yourself in Jesus' place as he attempts to explain the meaning of the miracle he performed.

Imagine yourself on a cool evening, sitting outside your house with your brothers and disciples gathered around you. Above you, stars dance against a dark sky. As you sit together, you watch the moon rise and hear the sound of insects.

As Jesus, you look into the eyes of curious followers. They question you about the water that became wine. They want to know the source of your power. They want you to explain your ability to perform miracles. Most of all, though, they want to know if you can use your unusual power to change the parts of their lives that are flat, colorless, and inadequate.

You are filled with a sense of wonder and awe at the gift your heavenly father has granted you. Your heart bursts with excitement as you think of the endless possibilities that lie ahead.

The power of God is at hand at all times. He longs to transform your life with that power. What do you think God might want to do in your life right now?

Day 2
John 2:12-14

Today picture in your mind's eye how it must have been for Jesus to take the journey from Capernaum to Jerusalem for Passover. Imagine yourself as Jesus. Feel the eagerness as you walk the dusty roads to the celebration of your ancestors. Hear the laughter and bantering of your traveling companions.

Countless stories of your heritage fill your mind as you move into the Temple courts. This year, however, your mind is filled with another force—your call. Everything is different for you.

Once in Jerusalem, you stand in the Temple court, a place you know is to be set apart for the worship of your father. You look around and see more clearly than ever before the men selling cattle, sheep, and doves. You are struck by the awareness that there aren't enough animals in the world to atone for the sins of the worshipers who are thronging into the Temple courts.

You walk over to the money-changers' tables and see how they cheat the pilgrims without any sense of shame or guilt. Your stomach lurches when you watch them snicker and wink when they cheat a poor man out of his last coin. You flinch when the raucous laughter penetrates your soul.

How can this go on? How long can these people believe that the shedding of the blood of animals will move them closer to God? How can the thieves and robbers live with themselves year after year?

What is it in your life that is unbecoming of a child of God?

Day 3
John 2:12-16

It's back into the Temple courts today. As Jesus, stand in the center of a place where wrong and evil are being flaunted as everyday commodities. Look around you. At every point someone is desecrating that which was meant to be holy. Hear the sounds of irreverence. Be revolted at the cacophony of sacrilege.

Feel the anger building inside you, starting deep within your body. Imagine its white-hot force growing stronger and stronger. You restrain yourself, but the righteous fury mounts.

When you breathe, the stench of animals and people crowded together fills your nostrils. Your disgust at the odors, however, is nothing to compare with the revulsion you feel toward the abuse of human beings in the name of religion.

Always connected intimately to your father, you seek His immediate guidance and direction. You know that He abhors what is happening in the Temple courts. You know that He wants His children to have a better way of life than what is perpetuated at this observance. You listen for the still, sure voice and as always, you hear it.

See yourself pick up a rope. Pull its length through your hands. Feel the sting of it on your palms. Suddenly, all the power of your anger comes together and explodes through your arms. You pull your arm back and swing the whip down into the midst of the tables, overturning them and sending animals and coins and people flying.

How has God used force to get your attention and change you?

Day 4
John 2:12-17

What about those times when you start something that is bigger than you had imagined, but once into it, you must see it through to the end? What about those moments when you see that your actions are going to change others' perceptions of you?

Did Jesus wonder about what others might think of his behavior in the Temple courts? Did it cross his mind that he might be getting himself in trouble with his anger? Did he wish he could take back what he had done?

Put yourself in the scene in the Temple courts. You are now the center of attention; all eyes are focused on you.

Hear the screams and curses as the owners of the animals leap to catch frightened creatures. Hear the sounds of the confused animals. Listen to the coins rattling across the stone floors and the loud voices of the moneychangers as they scamper to retrieve their precious money.

Angry voices demand explanations. Who do you think you are? What are you doing? Who gave you the authority to do this?

Still other voices shout threats and call your name. You are crazy. I'll get you. You'll pay for this.

Out of the corner of your eye you spot your disciples. Horrified, they huddle in a corner. You hear them quoting scripture to each other. You know that this experience will provide an important moment of instruction. While you may appear to be out of control, you are actually under the control of God.

Has God acted in your life in a way you didn't understand?

Day 5
John 2:12-22

Recall a time when you had to face up to the consequences of what you had done. Remember a moment when you had to meet, eye to eye, someone to whom you would account for your deeds.

Meet Jesus at the precise moment today back in the Temple courts. Imagine yourself standing in the middle of utter chaos. Picture yourself standing very still, holding the whip of cords in your hands, your eyes blazing with wrath. See yourself meeting the eyes of each person directly; you don't flinch in the face of their rage toward you.

From the corner of the Temple courts some of the leaders of the Jews emerge. The fire in their eyes is no match for that which burns in yours. Hear their rage when they ask you to tell them who ordered you to do such a thing.

Look at them, defenders of their faith! Look deep into their eyes. Although they have participated in the abuses of the Temple worship, you pity them. Even though they have taken their cut from the profits, you see them with eyes of compassion.

Carefully listening for your father's guidance, you answer them, but you don't give them the answer they expect. Nor do they, with their limited vision, understand your answer. You move their attention to the real issue.

With your answer, too, you give them a hint about who they are. If they have eyes to see and ears to hear, they will realize that you are giving them important information.

When has an ending opened up for you the way for a new beginning?

Day 6
John 2:12-23

Recall a time when you expended a great deal of emotion. Perhaps you expressed the emotion openly, as Jesus did in the cleansing of the Temple. On the other hand, you may have kept it locked inside you. However you experienced those deep emotions, your body registered the aftershocks.

Using the gift of imagination, see yourself as Jesus, walking down the steps of the Temple courts. You walk over to the disciples and attempt to look into the eyes of each one. Some meet your gaze; others look at their feet or beyond you to the Temple, looming grandly behind you.

You notice how weary your body is now. You long for a drink of water and a place to sit, away from the stares of the crowd. One of the disciples follows you; you don't know which one or which of them want to be seen with you.

Steadily, you walk on. Your labored breathing relaxes as you take deep breaths. You wipe your brow with your sleeve. Looking down, you see animal blood on your sandals and feet.

You turn around and call the disciples to follow. Quietly, they speed up their steps and sit down with you on the grass. Their questions penetrate the silence. Voluntarily, you make yourself accountable to them because you have brought them into your life.

The Living Christ allows experiences we cannot understand. He reveals his reasoning on his timetable. What experiences are you still waiting to understand?

Day 7
John 2:2-25

For today imagine yourself as Jesus at the Passover Feast in Jerusalem. You are participating in all of the rituals and ceremonies. You are busy with the activities of the observance. Whatever you do, you enter fully into life.

Here and there, as the Father directs you, you perform miracles and give evidence of the divine power that flows unhindered from the Father through you. Always the miraculous signs are meant to show the power of the Father. Always that power is intended for the good of people.

More than anything you want people to know that your purpose is to reveal God. Your intent is to show God's loving and kind nature. You also want them to see His grace at work through you.

What is it like for you as you make your way through the crowds to see people pointing at you and whispering behind their hands? How do you feel when individuals approach you and beg for a miracle? What is your response when "hangers-on" want to be with you, not because they love you or want to learn from you, but merely because they want to bask in your reflected glory? How do you handle those who would use you for their own benefit?

You are constantly aware that the disciples are watching. You want them to know that you answer only to your father. You receive your instructions only from Him. You are playing your life to an audience of one, the only audience that matters.

To whom do you answer? To whom are you playing your life?

152

UNWRAPPING SOULS

Raising Lazarus

John 11:1-44

Day 1

John 11:1-44

The action of this passage centers around the family of Lazarus of Bethany and his sisters Mary and Martha, all of whom are close friends of Jesus. Jesus has been a dinner guest in their home and, apparently, they feel close enough to him to call for him immediately when Lazarus becomes ill.

Imagine yourself as Jesus, going about your work in another town. You are busy with the needs of many people. They are pulling you, demanding your attention, and wanting you to spend time with them. Furthermore, the controversy around your work is growing.

Put yourself in that dreaded moment when a messenger appears to tell you that your friend is sick. You hear the words about your friend and the urgency in the messenger's voice. You see the worry etched in his face.

Feel the tug in Jesus' heart as he stands in the terrible dilemma of needing to be in two places at one time. Feel the competing needs, those right in front of you and those of your dear friends far away. Imagine the frustration of priorities at war with each other.

Connected intimately with his heavenly father, Jesus knows the outcome for Lazarus. He also knows that this messenger and his friend may not have the same assurance.

When you are caught in opposing priorities, how do you discern the difference between the urgent and the important?

Day 2
John 11:1-44

What was Jesus thinking when he delayed going to his friends immediately? How on earth could he put their urgent need on hold for two days? One would think that being Jesus' close friends would have some benefit, especially in crisis.

Imagine what must have been going on in Jesus' mind and heart during those two days he tarried, taking care of his own business while his friends were in grave trouble. He was confident of what he was doing, but he also must have known that others couldn't know his heart and intent.

Consider the risk Jesus took with his friends by waiting to go to Lazarus. Consider still another risk he took by going back to Judea where the religious authorities were lying in wait for him. Imagine what it was like for him to be misunderstood by his friends and to be at the center of controversy.

With the heart of Jesus, feel what it is like to be misunderstood no matter what you do. With his compassion, feel what it is like to want to serve humankind, open blind eyes, set prisoners free, and liberate people to live in the center of the Father's love, only to be misconstrued and held in suspicion. How must that have been for Jesus?

What do you do when you try to do the right thing, believing you are being led by God, but you are not understood? How do you handle having your motives questioned?

155

Day 3

John 11:1-44

Picture yourself as Jesus, walking along a dusty road toward Bethany. See the disciples, especially Thomas, walking with you. Feel the tension in the air as they discuss whether or not you should go where you are in danger.

As Jesus, you pray as you go, staying connected to the Heavenly Father. You breathe deeply, centering yourself in the presence of God wherever you are. You savor the sights and sounds of nature and enjoy the companionship of your disciples, especially in this tense time. You know the disciples cannot see the plan, but you hope they trust your heart.

At the outskirts of Bethany a messenger approaches and tells you Lazarus is already dead. Is that a tone of censure you hear in his voice?

Suddenly your friend Martha comes running to meet you. You notice the strained expression on her face. It is as if she has aged ten years since you last saw her. You know how much she loved her brother.

You notice also that Mary is not with her. You know that you will have to explain your reasons and your ways to her.

At the very instant Martha reaches you, she begins to chastise you. You understand her distress. You know that she had counted on you. You wanted her to count on you.

You reach for her, but she holds herself back from you. You feel the anger and tension in her body. You struggle to maintain your composure. This is a big event for both of you.

How do you feel when you know that you have let someone down?

Day 4

John 11:1-44

Reenter the scene for today's meditation in the moment when Jesus and Martha stand face to face. Feel the strain between them as Martha accuses her friend of letting her down. Feel the strength in Jesus as he stands firm on the truth.

Imagine yourself as Jesus, looking into Martha's face. Feel her grief with her; after all, Lazarus was your friend, too.

You know that this moment is one of the most significant moments of your ministry. You know there is a picture that is much bigger than you can see from your present vantage point and that as you obey the guidance of your father, more people than just Lazarus will be changed.

Hear your words to Martha about her brother's resurrection. See the impatience in her face and the edge to her voice when she comes back at you. While you sense her frustration, you are also aware of the crowd that has gathered around you. You open your mind and heart more fully to the guidance of your father.

Hear your words about resurrection. Hear yourself naming yourself the Resurrection and Life. As you do, you see more clearly than before into your own future. At the same time you see even better what it means for your followers to "die to self." The mysteries of life, death, and resurrection begin to take sharper focus in your own mind. In this moment you know yourself and your purpose more clearly.

What does it mean to you that Jesus is the Resurrection and the Life?

Day 5

John 11:1-44

With the God-given ability and creative power to see with the mind's eye, re-create this dramatic scene in your imagination. Stop the action, in your mind, as Jesus is talking to Martha. Imagine what it is like for Jesus to be able to comfort with his words and presence.

Picture yourself as Jesus watching Martha turn from you and move quickly back toward the house. You see Mary, her sister, standing in the shadows, looking at you from a distance. You meet the eyes of the woman you know well, and your heart aches because she doesn't understand and thinks you have let her down. You see Martha whisper to Mary.

Watch Mary run to you. Feelings tumble faster and faster in you as she comes to you and falls at your feet. The mourners wail louder, but all you hear are her plaintive words, "If only you had been here." Your heart wrenches.

Hear your voice when you ask where Lazarus has been buried. See Mary sobbing at your feet.

Suddenly you cannot contain your own feelings. Caught in the grips of this family drama, you begin to weep. Feel your own grief, Jesus. You, the Lord of all of life, experience the full range of human emotion. You, Son of Man, overflow with sorrow and frustration.

What does it do to your concept of God to see Jesus weeping? How does it feel to know that he wept for his friends? Does he weep for you?

Day 6

Begin today's meditation by experiencing the intensity of Jesus' emotion as he walked quickly to the hillside cave, the burial place of Lazarus. With Jesus, hear the accusations swirling around you. You know the skepticism. You are aware that no one understands the full picture of your actions or reads the motivation of your heart.

Hear your voice commanding someone, anyone, to roll away the stone. With your body, feel the shockwaves that shoot through the crowd. You know that you are violating ancient laws, but you stay the course. You know what you are doing.

You hear Martha protest. You turn and look right into her eyes, your own eyes blazing power and energy. You ask her if she didn't hear you, and then you make your command again.

You raise your eyes to the heavens. You and your father are in perfect accord. It is deathly quiet. Are the people experiencing horror? Or is it awe? Are they frightened out of their wits? Or are they on tip-toe with expectation?

"Come forth, Lazarus!" Your voice booms out into the stillness of the moment.

What is it like for you, Jesus, to command life out of death, blessing from curse, wholeness out of illness, gain from loss, victory out of defeat? What do you feel when you give life?

Is there a part of you that has died? What is it like to hear Jesus call to that part of you, "Come forth"?

Day 7

John 11:1-44

Today imagine the moment when the words of Jesus, "Come forth!" echoed out across the landscape. What would it have been like to have uttered those words? How would it have felt to have been Jesus and have had life-giving power? Our finite imaginations can take us only so far into the life of Jesus, but we know that it must have been awesome.

Picture yourself as Jesus, standing at the opening of the hillside tomb. Experience the moment when Lazarus appears at the entrance of the tomb, fully wrapped in graveclothes. Hear the startled gasps of the people around you. Notice the shock on their faces. Be aware of Mary and Martha looking at you and then at their brother, stunned and overjoyed.

Hear yourself commanding the people to unwrap Lazarus, knowing full well that you are asking them to defy convention and break the strict ceremonial laws of their religion even to touch one who has been dead. Hear the authority in your voice.

This is your way, isn't it, Jesus? From this time forward the community of faith will be asked to participate in each other's "unwrapping." Within the mystical body of Christ, folks will be asked to help each other come unbound from fear, guilt, shame, inferiority, hatred, and anger. The church will be asked to help you set each other free.

What part of you is wrapped in graveclothes? Who can help you come unbound? Who do you need to help come unbound?

KNOW MY COMPASSION

When God became man in the person of Jesus of Nazareth, He chose to take on human form and to identify fully with humankind. Even though God could have avoided experiencing the full range of human emotion, He chose to know what it was to live as a human being with human limitations.

Because of his complete identification with humankind, Jesus had an understanding of the frailties of people. Because he lived in community with a real family and had real friends, he had the capacity to comprehend the struggles of everyday life and to grapple with complex issues for which there are no easy answers.

Because he was God, Jesus had the capacity to see straight through to the heart of a person. Regardless of what was going on in the life of someone or what they might be doing, Jesus always related to them with sensitivity. He always wanted the best for the people whose lives he touched.

Having compassion toward people involves having empathy for their situations. Having compassion means that you look at people through eyes of mercy and grace. Compassion takes the edge off your condemnation and gives you the grace to see each person through the lenses of love. Let the compassionate God give you His tender mercy. Then extend that compassion out into the life of someone you know.

FRIENDS HELPING FRIENDS
Healing the Paralytic

Mark 2:1-12

Day 1
Mark 2:1-12

Create the scene in this story in your imagination. What kind of house is in Capernaum? Who is Jesus' host? What time of day is it?

Picture the room where Jesus is standing to teach. What size is it? Where is he positioned? How many people are there? Imagine how it is for him to teach people who really want to learn.

Put yourself in Jesus' shoes. Imagine how it makes his heart sing to know that the people are there because they want to be. How liberating it must be for him to experience their open minds and hearts. What a pleasure it is to provide answers for people who really want answers, to help honest seekers find what they are looking for, and to make the deepest truth about life with your father available to those who have knocked on the door of this house.

As Jesus, you respond to the various questions and enjoy the way that one question leads to another. It is as if all of you are peeling layer after layer of truth, exploring the mysteries of God together. Feel the satisfaction of connecting with other seekers in this way.

As you look around the room, you notice every person. Every individual is important to you. Every life is worth your life. How does it feel to you to be so intimately connected?

Do you take your mission in life and your work for God seriously?

Day 2

Mark 2:1-12

On this day re-create the picture of the crowded room. Imagine that all the energy in the room is directed toward Jesus; all conditions are right for him to do his work.

In that open and free environment Jesus feels and knows the powerful, intimate connection to his father. It is as if all the lines between father and son are clear. He also feels the strong connection with the individuals in the room. Imagine how good it must have felt to be open to the Father and to the people at the same time.

As Jesus, you are aware of a slight commotion outside the front door. You can see that there are some men who are carrying another man on a pallet, but you can't see the whole scene because of the crowd of people.

Suddenly you hear a sound from above and look up. You cannot believe your eyes. One by one the tiles of the roof are removed, exposing the faces of four men. You stand there, looking up into the faces of men who are looking down at you.

You watch, surprised and moved with compassion, as the men lower their friend on the pallet in front of you. You look into the invalid's face; he looks into yours. You look back at his friends and hear a quiet, holy hush fall over the room. What will you do? What are you thinking? What do you feel?

Are you willing to go to any length to meet Jesus face to face?

Day 3
Mark 2:1-12

Re-create the scene in the crowded room. Connect with the action just as the four friends lower the ailing man through the roof and place him in front of Jesus.

At this dramatic moment all eyes are directed to the face of Jesus. Stunned by the audacity of the four friends, some people snicker nervously. Still others whisper about the roof being dismantled. A few stare at the paralytic lying on the floor.

Frankly, you, as Jesus, are more than a little curious. This has never happened to you before. What is it about these friends that made them go to such lengths to get this man to you?

You want to ask them what they have been through with this friend. Is it true for them that "desperate times require desperate solutions?" Have they suffered long with their friend?

As Jesus, you look up into the faces of the men who have brought their friend to you. You see etched on each face simple trust that moves you deeply. You know that they have complete faith in your ability to make their friend whole.

When you look into their faces, you see a childlike trust that made them understand that if they would do their part in getting their friend to you, you would do the rest. In the quiet strength of these four men, peering down at you through the roof, you see deep compassion.

What part of you needs to take to Jesus? What friend can you "take to him" in prayer?

Day 4

Mark 2:1-12

Put yourself in the shoes of Jesus. Get in touch with his tender, compassionate heart. As you look at the paralytic and his friends, you wish everyone had friends who were willing to appear absurd if it would help their loved one. You wish all people had others who would be willing to go to ridiculous lengths so that someone else might encounter you. You wish others would have the boldness to interrupt whatever you were doing to take care of the friend they loved.

Imagine yourself as Jesus in the crowded room, looking up at those four friends. Then you turn your attention to the man on the mat. Is he embarrassed? Is he self-conscious? Is he in physical pain? Did he want to come to you, or is he there only on the faith of his friends?

What you see when you look into the eyes of the paralytic is a man who has nothing to lose. You see years of turmoil and pain, and when you look deep into his soul, you know that separation from God is at the core of his problem.

You turn to the kingdom of God within and ask your father for guidance and power. You hear your voice, gentle but firm, telling the man that his sins are forgiven. From now on, he doesn't have to be separated from God; he doesn't have to bear the results of the separation in his frozen limbs.

What need does Jesus need to meet for you? How does he want to use you to meet the needs of others?

Day 5

Mark 2:1-12

Join the uproar in the crowded room in the instant when Jesus declares the paralytic's sins forgiven. Hear the outrage of the teachers of the law. Sense the rage and fury, all directed toward Jesus.

With Jesus, feel the conflict between meeting individual, human need and setting a man free of a physical prison, knowing that you have set yourself up for a great deal of trouble with the religious establishment. Feel the tug of war that pulls you between the old and the new. Hear the accusations of the on-lookers. Hear the Father's voice telling you that you have done the right thing. Hear them almost spit the word "blasphemy." Hear your father remind you that people have priority over law and that human need is more important than religious precedent.

Hear the strength in your voice as you stand up to the challenges of the religious leaders, both those spoken and unspoken. Hear yourself claim the authority your father has given you, an authority that is yours alone. Hear the outrage escalate as you strike at the very heart of Jewish belief.

As Jesus, you pull your attention away from the uproar and return it to the man on the pallet. His eyes dart from you to the others, and you sense his fear. How vulnerable he looks, lying on the mat.

Do you allow or inhibit the healing power of Jesus? Do you participate with Jesus in the work of grace or stop it?

Day 6

Mark 2:1-12

What is it like when conflict takes over a room? How does it feel to be at the center of conflict? Does it help to know that you are right? Does knowing that you are within the will of God make the slings and arrows of others' censure more bearable?

Picture Jesus, standing in the very heat of the battle, the lame man lying at his feet. Imagine the hostility in peoples' faces; hear their angry tones. Always, though, you feel Jesus' magnificent serenity and composure, no matter how hot the battle. In all times he is calm and cool because he is always in union with his father.

Imagine what it was like for Jesus to have the power to turn to the paralytic and command him to get up off his mat and walk. Imagine yourself as Jesus, reaching down to the man.

See the man reach his own frail arm up and grasp you by the hand. Imagine how it would be for the healing energy of God Almighty to surge through your body and into the broken body of the man on the mat. Experience the ecstasy Jesus surely must have felt when the man did, in fact, stand up, straight and whole.

As Jesus, you know that the proof of a teacher or prophet is in the results. You think that you can hear your heart singing as this man stoops over and picks up his mat and begins walking away.

Are you willing to be God's instrument in the healing of others?

Day 7
Mark 2:1-12

As Jesus, you stand in the crowded room. You are aware that God's grace and glory have just surged through you into the physical body of a paralytic and that the man is now walking out the door with his mat rolled up under his arm.

You are also aware that the four friends on the roof scramble away from their lookout and race each other to the steps leading up to the roof. You hear them shouting to their friend. He shouts back, "Look at me. Look at me walk. That man from Nazareth has healed me."

You close your eyes and pray that the man will know that the real healing occurred at the inner core of his being where you have forgiven his sins. You hope that he knows what has been on the inside has been manifested on the outside. This was a man frozen in the sin of fear, guilt, and shame. This was a man whose outer reality was a reflection of his inner brokenness, and you have made that right. If only he will stay right with your father, all will be well for him.

Standing there, you hear the whispers of the witnesses of this grand event. You know that they are amazed and cannot argue with what they have seen with their own eyes. You hear them praising God. You pray that they will always know that all healing is ultimately from the hand of your father.

What was it like for Jesus to be in the center of such competing forces? What was it like for him to set people free?

Have you ever felt empowered by God for a specific act of mercy?

THE HEM OF HIS GARMENT
Healing a Suffering Woman

Mark 5:21-43

Day 1
Mark 5:21-24

With your creative mind, visualize a crowd gathered by the lake. See Jesus stepping out of a boat onto dry land and the people rushing to crowd around him.

With his ears, hear the voices calling to him, each wanting his attention. See the hands reaching for him, trying to touch him. Imagine what it was like to be in the middle of human need and in the center of controversy. How do you choose whose need you will meet first? How do you decide whose problem is the greatest, except by the guidance of your heavenly father?

Suddenly you see a man push through the crowd toward you. You recognize him as one of the synagogue rulers. You speak to him, calling him by name, and he falls at your feet.

See yourself as Jesus, stooping down to hear the plea of this distraught father, pleading with you to come home with him. Hear his anguish as he tells you that his child, his precious daughter, is desperately ill.

When you look at Jairus, you know that it has cost him to come to you. You realize that he has walked right out on the razor's edge of risk to seek your healing touch. Your heart goes out to him. You know now where you are to go. In this fervent plea of Jairus you have your direction from your father.

Do you rely on the Living Christ to set your priorities? Do you let him guide you to "the next thing indicated"?

Day 2

Mark 5:24-29

Put yourself in the place of Jesus, using the gift of your imagination. Feel the connection between yourself and Jairus, who feels despair at the threat of losing his daughter. Feel the energy of commitment to helping this man in need. Experience the moment when you know for sure where your father wants you to do your work.

You start moving through the crowd. Even as you move toward Jairus, others begin calling your name, pleading with you to meet their needs. You are pressed on every side by human need, yet you are choosing to follow this one man to his home.

You see women, bent over with years of pain. Here and there a child with a twisted limb or a cleft palate reaches for you. Men, blind and lame and covered with sores, call your name. You are assaulted on every side by the sights, sounds, and smells of sickness and brokenness. Yet you choose to follow this one man to his home.

You hear the shouts of one of your followers, urging the people to let you walk through the crowd. But the shouts fall on deaf ears. The needs of the people make them throw ordinary courtesy and caution to the wind. They need you.

Suddenly, something happens. You feel energy leave you. It is as if someone has pulled a plug and your power has drained from you. Someone has touched you ever so slightly.

Are you so attuned to the Father's guidance that you can sense His slightest whisper, gentlest touch, and smallest gesture?

173

Day 3

Mark 5:24-31

Take a few moments to put yourself back in the push and pull of the noisy crowd. As Jesus, feel the press of humanity against you. Sense the despair of human need and the smell of desperation.

Reenter this scene at the moment when the woman with a condition of hemorrhaging reaches out desperately through the crowd and touches the hem of Jesus' robe.

Move into the experience of Jesus at the moment when he senses that the power and energy have gone out of him. As if you were in his shoes, see yourself stop suddenly and search the crowd.

Hear your voice ask the disciples, "Who touched me?" Hear their frustration when they respond, "With this crowd, how could we know?"

With your penetrating eyes and compassionate heart, guided always by your heavenly father, you search the crowd until your eyes fall on a woman. Trembling, she falls to her knees in front of you.

See yourself stoop down so that you can hear her faltering words. She won't look at you; she keeps her eyes diverted. You see her tears falling to the ground. You hear her confession, and your heart aches. What suffering this woman has endured. What terrible pain and frustration this child of God has had.

Do you believe that the Living Christ is as sensitive to your need as the human Jesus was to this woman? If not, why not?

Day 4
Mark 5:25-34

Use your imagination to re-create the scene in the crowd. Pick up the action in the moment when the woman with the long-term illness falls at the feet of Jesus.

As Jesus, you strain to hear the woman's words. The crowd continues to press around you, shouting and pleading with you for healing. The woman, ashamed and scared, keeps her head bowed, so you must lean down to hear her story.

There, in the crowd, you listen to the confession of this woman, shamed for years because of her condition. You take in all she says. Even more, you listen with your heart, sensing the emotional pain she has carried with the physical pain. Your heart breaks when you think of all the wasted years when she could have been enjoying life and making a difference in the lives of her family and friends.

You listen to the ways she has sought help, but always in vain. You frown when you realize that she has spent a fortune seeking healing. This is not a person who has stood back, waiting for someone else to do for her. This is not a woman who has been passive about doing what she needed to do for herself.

This is a woman who has taken initiative, only to be frustrated time after time. This is a woman who was willing to risk censure, rebuke, and further shame to press through the crowds to you. This is a woman of faith.

What would you be willing to risk to make contact with Jesus?

175

Day 5
Mark 5:25-34

If you had been Jesus, stooping down to hear the woman's confession in the midst of a noisy crowd, what would you have felt? Would you have cared what others thought about you?

If you had paused to pay attention to a woman who had reached out for you while a Jewish leader waited for you to help him, would you have been worried?

Would it have bothered you to spend time with one person while the crowd needed you? What would your heart have told you about that one woman?

View the scene as Jesus might have seen it. Visualize the small woman, kneeling in front of you. Sense the smells of the crowd, pushing around you. See the faces of the serious seekers and of the merely curious.

Summoning the power of your heavenly father, you open yourself fully to be His instrument of healing. Yielding to His will, you let yourself be used as a physician once again.

Hear yourself call this woman, "Daughter." Feel the love in your heart as you speak gently to her.

Hear yourself tell the woman that her faith in you has healed her. See the expression on her face when she finally has the courage to lift her face and look into yours. In that moment you know that she is healed, and so does she.

When you look into her face, you see the face of all women everywhere. Your heart goes out to this woman and to all women.

Your wound is the doorway through which Jesus can walk to you. Are you willing to let him walk through the doorway?

Day 6
Mark 5:21-36

On this day see yourself moving through all the action in this passage. Imagine yourself as Jesus in each frame. Imagine how he feels with each encounter.

See yourself as Jesus, still speaking to the woman. Feel the intensity of her faith in you. She has staked everything on the belief that she can find healing in you.

As you talk quietly with her, several men push through the crowd and break into your conversation with the woman. Shouting, they tell Jairus the bad news. He looks frantically at you.

Moving from one crisis to another, you keep yourself centered in the presence of your heavenly father. You listen to Him, and He tells you what to say and do.

"All is well," you tell Jairus. He looks at you in disbelief, but follows you to his house.

You motion for Peter, James, and John to follow you and signal the other disciples to wait behind.

You walk quickly toward the house of Jairus. He follows alongside, weeping. You know he believes that if you had not tarried, you could have saved his daughter. You feel his blame and accusations, but you see a bigger picture.

Imagine what is in the heart of Jesus as he walks up to the house where the mourners are already wailing. Is he on trial, or are the people?

What is it like for you when you feel that Jesus is not on task with your problem? How do you keep yourself centered in him?

Day 7
Mark 5:35-43

At times Jesus sought out people who were in need of his healing. At other times he simply came across people in need. Sometimes he waited for people to come to him. He healed some from a distance and laid his hands on other persons who were ill. Always his healing gave glory to his heavenly father. Never did he try to draw attention to himself.

On this day imagine yourself as Jesus, bounding up the steps to the house of Jairus amidst accusations on the one hand and wailing and mourning on the other. In the midst of all this you must deal with the disciples' confusion about what you are doing. You must teach them well.

You walk into the child's room and move confidently to her bedside. Without hesitation, you take her by the hand and tell her to get up. You watch with delight as the life-force floods her tiny body and she sits up in her bed. You enjoy the sheer ecstasy on the faces of her mother and father. You are especially pleased that the disciples had a chance to see what your father can do through a willing instrument.

Hear your voice tell the people who have seen this miracle that they are to keep it to themselves. Then, getting practical, you tell the child's family to feed her.

Feel the gratification of knowing that you are doing exactly what your heavenly father wants you to do.

Are you doing what the Heavenly Father wants you to do?

REVERSING ROLES
Washing Feet

John 13:1-17

Day 1

John 13:1-17

What an amazing thing it is that the Lord of life, whose very work was motivated by his passionate love for the whole world, also loved individuals. Jesus of Nazareth, God Himself, had deep, intimate relationships. He who loved the world and gave himself for it also loved individuals lavishly.

Imagine yourself as Jesus, sitting at dinner late in the evening. You are with your closest friends. You are connected to each of them in a deep, abiding way. You sense that your relationship with them is about to change and that they do not yet fully understand the impact of your presence with them or your purpose for them. For tonight, however, you simply want to enjoy being with these friends.

Picture the scene on this special occasion. Inhale the aromas of food and taste the wine. See gentle candlelight flicker on the faces of your friends. Hear their conversations as they relax in the evening with each other.

Your heart is filled with gratitude for these friends. You give thanks, silently and fervently, for the capacity to have friends. You know that your life on earth is blessed because you have entered into the sacred realm of holy friendship with these specific people.

Who are your dearest friends? Do you spend quality time with them? Are you a good friend of Christ's? If not, why not?

Day 2

John 13:1-17

To study the life of Jesus is to study a life of composure and serenity. This was a man who was completely at home with himself because he knew who he was and what he was to do with his life. Furthermore, he clearly understood that as long as he was fully abiding in and connecting with the Father, he was where he was supposed to be. This was a man who was sure of himself, sure enough to take on the demeanor and clothing of a servant.

Picture yourself as Jesus. The evening meal is finished. You and your disciples are seated around low tables, talking in hushed voices to each other.

You know exactly what you want to do to give the disciples a picture of what true servanthood means. In spite of all your teaching, they still think that leadership is about power over others, dominance, and rule. You know just the visual image you want to leave with them to help them understand the true nature of leadership.

Quietly, you stand up and walk over to the side of the room. You take off your outergarment and put on an apron. Some of the disciples turn to watch you, puzzled. Others continue their conversations, oblivious to the fact that they are about to see something amazing.

You pour water from a pitcher into the basin. It reminds you of the woman at the well and the Living Water that you are.

Are you secure enough in yourself to serve others?

Day 3
John 13:1-17

Imagine the hush that falls over the room when Jesus approaches the disciples with a basin and towel. Imagine that a servant rushes over to take the task away from Jesus by reaching for the basin and towel. See yourself as Jesus, motioning the servant away. This is an optimal teaching moment, and you don't want to miss the opportunity.

Place yourself in the heart of Jesus as he kneels down before the first disciple. Picture yourself putting the basin on the cool stone floor. Hear someone whisper, "Jesus, what are you doing?"

You smile to yourself. You have grown accustomed to astonishing these men. You like the element of surprise. There is something about surprise that opens minds and hearts to amazing possibilities.

See yourself reach for the feet of your friend. You sense his resistance as you lovingly and gently wash his feet. You dry them with the towel, but you keep your head down because your eyes overflow with tears just as your heart overflows with love.

You move to the next disciple and kneel again on the stone floor. If it is possible, the room grows even more quiet and still. It is as if no one is breathing. All eyes are focused on you.

When has someone done something for you that was such a basic primal gesture that you were embarrassed, but also touched deeply?

Day 4
John 13:1-17

Reenter today's meditation as Jesus in the cool, darkened room where Jesus is washing the feet of the disciples. Hear the sound of the water as it falls back down into the basin from the foot of each man. Feel the roughness of the towel. Taste the saltiness of tears that roll down your face.

With the heart of Jesus, feel the deep love and compassion you have for each man. Let your love for each one pass gently from your hands to his feet and up into his whole being. Connect with each one, heart to heart.

Imagine how it feels to kneel before big, burly Peter. See yourself, as Jesus, reaching for his foot, only to see him recoil in resistance. Look into his face as you reach again for his foot. You see his horror. You hear his protests.

Gently, you tell him how things must be. Firmly, Peter argues with you. You feel the tension in the air, but remain calm. You know Peter and his heart. You know what will reach him, so you tell him again how things must be.

You admire Peter's strong will. You need someone like this to carry on your work. You know that Peter can't be bought. You also know that he must learn the humility of letting someone else serve him.

You insist and stand your ground. Peter is not accustomed to giving up or giving in.

Is there a part of you that is resistant to being served?

Day 5

John 13:1-17

For today revisit the scene in the upper room, beginning with the moment Jesus stood up and walked over to the basin and pitcher. Make every detail sharp and clear in your imagination. Put yourself in the scene as Jesus.

Feel the water on your hands and feel the weight of Peter's feet as you hold them. Imagine yourself blotting the water with the rough towel.

You are keenly aware of the impact Peter's surrender to this act of servanthood is having on the other disciples. You feel their eyes taking in every movement you make. You also know that it is costing Peter dearly to let you do this; his pride and self-sufficiency are legendary.

What would you have felt when you held Peter's foot in your hands? What would have been in your heart when you stood your ground with Peter and laid out the terms of having a relationship with you? How would your felt-sense have shifted in the moment when Peter finally understood? Would you have smiled when Peter finally surrendered and entered into the humility of true servanthood?

Imagine yourself bending over Peter's feet. See every part of those feet. Think about the miles he has walked and the miles he will walk for you and your work. Feel the roughness of the skin; you know that the rough exterior masks a gentle, tender heart. Feel the love in your heart for this one human being.

When did you last do something very ordinary for a loved one?

Day 6

John 13:1-17

Pick up the action of this scene at the point when Jesus has washed the feet of every disciple, ending with Peter.

Put yourself in Jesus' place as he stands, picks up the basin and towel, and walks over to the side of the room. See a servant take the basin and towel and leave the room with them.

If you could think like Jesus, imagine what would have been going on in your mind as you put on your outergarment. What would you have been feeling as you walked back over to the table and took your place with the disciples.

See yourself sit down. Take a drink of wine. Look around the table and into the eyes of each man. Will they meet your gaze, or will they drop their eyes, uncomfortable in the intensity of the moment.

You long for them to understand the full impact of what you have done, so you ask them one by one if they understand. You tell them that you have done this deed because you love them so much. You explain servant leadership to them and tell them how much difference humility makes in leading other people.

Sit in silence with these men. Let the meaning of the moment rest in the silence between you. Breathe deeply, praying that the love your father has for each one will sink deeper and deeper into the recesses of each heart, transforming each life, drawing each person into union with you and with the Father.

What has the Living Christ done to show his love for you?

Day 7
John 13:1-17

In your imagination sit with Jesus and the disciples in the evening around the table. You have just washed their feet. You have explained to them the meaning of your actions. Now you are waiting for the impact of what you have done to sink in.

Finally you speak again. Hear the firmness of your voice in the still, somber room. "This is what you are to do for each other," you tell the disciples. "As I have washed your feet and done this menial task, so you are to do this for each other."

You look around the table at the strong, self-reliant men. You know that the picture of servanthood you have given them does not match their image of true leadership. You know that, for them, what you have done is more a picture of weakness and servitude than of strength and power. You realize that you are pushing them out to the edge of their own growth. You wonder how they will respond. The willingness to serve, in fact, is a necessary attribute of true leaders.

You see them look at each other. You know they are wondering how it will feel to perform such lowly tasks for each other. You know it is even harder for them to let themselves be washed and served by another. Pride falls hard.

You breathe deeply and move to the inner sanctuary with the Father. You and he join together in blessing these, your own.

What does humility mean to you? How good are you at practicing humility?

THE CHILD'S WAY
The Only Way

Mark 10:13-16
Matthew 18:1-6; 19:13-15
Luke 18:15-17

Day 1

Mark 10:13-16

In your mind's eye create a picture of today's scene. See yourself on a grassy hillside. As Jesus, you have been dealing with heavy issues with both serious seekers and the merely curious onlookers.

You have had to stay on your toes to respond to the questions that have come rapidly, one right after another. You have answered questions about divorce and greatness in the kingdom of God. You know the questions were provoked by the healing of the young boy who had an evil spirit.

There is a lull in the questions. You seek out a large stone. Imagine yourself sitting down on it. Feel its coolness beneath your hands. Stroke its rough places and think about all the forces of nature that have shaped it.

You take a few deep breaths and look up at a bird in a tree. You smile as it entertains you with a particularly joyful hymn. You watch a white cloud sneak across the blue sky. How good it is to walk and talk in your father's world.

Over to your left you see a young mother walking tentatively toward you. She is carrying an infant and holds a young girl by the hand. Ahead of her, a younger child toddles; he hasn't been up on those legs very long. The woman's older child walks a few paces behind her; he would rather be with his friends. You motion to her to bring her children to you.

The Living Christ is very fond of the little child within you. What feelings do you have about the childlike part of yourself?

Day 2

Mark 10:13-16

Return to the stone seat as Jesus. Use the powers of your imagination to paint the scene in your mind's eye. Include the green grass beneath your feet and the red and yellow wildflowers scattered across the meadow. Color in the brown and gray clothing of the people. Here and there someone wears a touch of purple or blue.

Notice how your spirits lift when you see the young mother approaching you with her children. Hear her older child ask her, "Why are we going to see him?"

"Because I want him to bless you," she answers. You smile because she knows that you have the ability to bless her children.

Out of the corner of your eye you notice another child approaching you. You stand up and hold out your arms to welcome all the children who will come to you. You can barely contain yourself. A smile pulls at the corners of your mouth. You can almost feel delight sparkling in your eyes.

You observe carefully every child, noting the unique characteristics of each one. Just as you are about to call out to one of the children whose name you know, one of your disciples pushes himself between you and the children. "Can't you see Jesus is tired?" he asks them, his voice stern.

You catch your breath and move out from behind the disciple to face him. This is a moment to teach children of all sizes.

The Living Christ loves the little child who still dwells within you. How do you stand in the way of his reaching that child?

189

Day 3

Mark 10:13-16

Imagine yourself as Jesus, standing with the disciples and the children. You recognize that your disciples have intervened out of loving motivation. They have seen how you have been challenged and questioned. They have compassion for you and concern for your physical state.

Feel the tension in the air. You can almost cut the silence that hangs over the children and their parents. You are aware of young eyes boring through you. You know that one must have the heart of a child to enter the kingdom of heaven.

Look into the eyes of your friend who is trying to take care of you. See beyond his sternness to the little boy inside him, a child who wants to be loved and accepted just as he is. See the yearnings that made him put his own life on the line to follow you to a place he doesn't know or quite understand.

Hear your voice, firm but kind, tell the disciples they must let the children come to you. Hear yourself explain to them that the children are a welcome break from the intellectual wrestlings with adults. Tell them that the innocence of children refreshes your spirit and that you want to be with the children, even now. Watch the expression of sternness turn to disbelief. Aren't children best left in the care of the women-folk?

Do you think the Living Christ prefers to spend time with the grown-up, polished you or with the natural, spontaneous child in you? Do you think it's possible that Christ loves both parts of you equally?

Day 4
Mark 10:13-16

Today visualize Jesus turning from the disciples to face the children who stand before you. Their eyes dart back and forth from one adult to the other, seeing all, but not understanding.

One of the children begins to cry; you watch her pull her mother's skirts around her, as if she could hide herself. A young boy breaks away and runs toward his friends. One of the children punches another, and the child kicks him. Children have a way of acting out the conflicts of adults.

Feel the smile return to your face as you observe the children. Stretch your arms toward them and tell them, "Come."

Your voice is the only cue the children need. Eager boys and girls scamper toward you. Each one works his way closer to you. They all want to touch you and to be touched by you.

A tiny girl, barely toddling, starts toward you but is knocked down by a larger child. You stoop to pick her up. Watch yourself swing her up in the air, laughing gleefully.

See yourself walk over to the large rock and sit down. The little girl nestles close to you, and the other children clamor for the place closest to you. An older child comes around and stands behind you, placing his hand on your shoulder.

"Don't you know," you call to your disciples, "that everyone needs at least one friend under five?"

For today, carry in your mind the vision of Jesus enjoying the presence of the children. Imagine how much he loves the little child in you. Do you love that child?

Day 5

Mark 10:13-16; Matthew 19:13-15

As you identify with Jesus today, place your attention back in the scene in the park. Re-create the sights and sounds of Jesus as he banters with the children. Imagine his reactions as the children pull on his arms and beg him to listen to them. Imagine how it feels for Jesus to know that the children feel perfectly safe with him.

As Jesus, become aware of the Heavenly Father's pleasure in every child. Listen carefully to His affirmation of all the children. He tells you that each one is unique. He knows what each child needs.

You put your finger under the chin of a little boy and tip his face up so that you can look in his brown eyes. Hear yourself as you speak his name. Watch yourself place your hands on his head and speak a prayer of blessing. Feel his hair on your hands. Sense the energy in the small lad.

Listening always to your father, you move your attention from one child to another, focusing intensely on each one as you bless him. Watch the children, eager for your blessing, push toward you.

See yourself take a crying baby from her mother and soothe her. Hear yourself croon the Father's love in her tiny ear. Hear yourself tell the mother that the Heavenly Father is joining her in nurturing and caring for this child; the Father, after all, loves the child even more than she and will watch over her all the days of her life.

Today imagine yourself being blessed by Jesus. Pass it on. Do you believe his blessing is for you?

Day 6

Matthew 18:1-6

As Jesus, see yourself standing in the village, talking with your disciples. Hear the sounds of laughter as villagers take care of their daily chores. Watch a little boy chasing a small lamb through the streets; hear his mother scold him.

Turn your attention now to the questions of the disciples. They are quizzing you about who will be the greatest in the kingdom of heaven. Feel your heart sink a bit. What will it take for these men to change their ideas about greatness? When will they understand that your kingdom is about a kind of power that is different from anything they have experienced before?

You listen to their questions and then look away from them. You discern guidance from the Father and know what to do. Your teaching aid appears in the form of a young boy.

Hear your voice as you call to the lad. See him throw down the stick he is carrying and race toward you. He greets you warmly and looks into your eyes with perfect trust and openness.

You place your hands on the boy's shoulders. Feel the rough fabric of his garment against your hands. He looks up at you and grins. You notice that his two front teeth are missing.

Slowly you turn the child around so that he faces the disciples. "This is the picture of what it means to be the greatest in the kingdom," you tell them.

You look into the disciples' eyes. Are they comprehending the truth?

What does the child in you know that the adult does not?

Day 7

Matthew 18:1-6; Luke 18:15-17

Re-create, with the gift of imagination, the moment when Jesus stands with the young lad and the disciples. Notice the silence in the adults as they attempt to understand the kingdom of God in a new way.

"A child's heart is open," you tell them. "You can only enter the Kingdom with a child's heart."

You look down at the boy. Notice the freshness in his expression. Feel the tug in your own heart as you ponder all he must endure in order to become a man.

Will there be strong men to guide this lad to maturity, or will the adults in his life destroy his spirit? Will some significant man teach him about the kingdom of heaven, or will someone put barriers in his journey to you? Who will love him as he needs to be loved? Will he have a worthy mentor?

Passion for life and for your father come out in the intensity of your words. You must impress on these disciples the importance of childlike trust. You must let them know how crucial it is that children be led to you. If the disciples are to learn anything, it must be the critical consequences of losing their childlike trust.

People believe that childlikeness is something to get over, like an infirmity. Your disciples must know that while it is important to grow out of childishness, maintaining childlike openness is a necessity in spiritual maturity.

Have you been trying to earn God's favor by being all grown up? Try opening your heart as a child and see what happens.

THE POWER OF ONE THING
Mary and Martha

Luke 10:38-41

Day 1

Luke 10:38-41

How did Jesus decide where he would stop for lunch as he traveled? Did he plan where he would spend the night? How did potential hosts spread the word that they would like to invite Jesus into their homes? Was it hard for him to work people into his busy schedule, or did he have plenty of time to be with people?

Use your imagination to picture Jesus, traveling through the countryside. See him enter the village of Bethany and walk into the center of town. Always guided by the wisdom, love, and will of his heavenly father, he moves from place to place.

On this day walk in Jesus' shoes toward the home of Mary, Martha, and Lazarus. See yourself walk up to a wide, covered porch. Imagine that there are flowers growing outside the house. Perhaps a wind chime hangs from the roof.

The door swings open, and Martha greets you, arms outstretched. You know that you are welcome in this home and will have the privilege of being there as part of the family. Hear the warmth and openness in Martha's voice. See the excitement in Mary's face as she scurries to greet you. Let yourself be embraced by gracious hosts and good friends.

What does it take to be a good friend of Jesus? How welcome is he in your private life?

Day 2
Luke 10:38-41

Putting yourself in the role of Jesus with your imagination, re-create the homey scene as Martha welcomes you and does all of the things a gracious hostess does to make you feel at home.

Smell the aroma of freshly baked bread. The smell of meat cooking outside wafts in through the open windows. You look into the dining room and see fresh flowers on the low table. You notice that one of the servants is pouring wine and preparing the serving utensils for a meal. From past experience you know that a meal prepared under Martha's directions will be a fine dining experience indeed.

As you sit down in your familiar chair, you look around the room. Everything is the same as you remember it. You sigh and settle back into the chair, comfortable in the home of your friends. Your disciples and some friends of the family gather around you and, as always, you begin to discuss the most important things about life with your father.

Your friend Mary sits down at your feet and smiles at you. You are so glad that she is close to you. Her heart is so open and eager, just like the heart of a child. Her mind is so quick and sharp, and her spirit is so tender and malleable. What a loving, available, ready disciple she is. She takes it all in, and you love her input in the conversation. Most of all, you love the fact that she loves to be with you.

Practice sitting with the Living Christ, just loving him. If you did this regularly, how might your life be different?

Day 3
Luke 10:38-41

Imagining that you can feel what Jesus felt, you reenter the scene in the home of Mary, Martha, and Lazarus. Experience the joy of being with friends and the challenge of intimate conversation about the most important things of life.

As Jesus, you are aware of the bustling in the dining room and kitchen. Out of the corner of your eye you see people move in and out of the room, carrying trays and pitchers, setting places, and carving meat.

Now and then you sense Martha's presence in the eating area. You hear her low voice as she directs the servants and corrects a child. Each time she enters the room you sense her anxiety level increasing. You know that she carries a lot of responsibility in this family. You also know that she has plenty of help in doing her duty.

You turn your attention toward Martha and notice the strain in her face. Your heart goes out to her. If only she could relax and lighten up a bit. You know, however, that her standards are high and that she wants you to have the best treatment of all.

As Jesus, you are keenly aware of family dynamics. You understand how things work among siblings. You have experienced the various parts each person plays within a family system, and you know how things can get tangled.

Is there a part of you that is Martha and a part that is Mary? Do you play one role to the exclusion of the other?

Day 4

Luke 10:38-41

On this day recall a time when you were doing all the work while others played or rested. How did you feel about that? Think about a time when you were doing what you wanted to do while other people were doing all the work. How was that for you? Remember a time when you got caught between two people who were at odds with each other. Imagine being Jesus in that position.

Use your abilities to visualize the scene in the home of Mary and Martha, entering at the moment when Martha has had enough of doing all the work while Mary sits at your feet. Picture the scene as Martha walks out of the dining room and challenges you, as Jesus, about the problem she is having with her sister.

Put yourself in Jesus' shoes as he looks back and forth between Martha and Mary. Imagine his feelings, as their honored guest, as he is drawn into their sibling problem. Imagine all the different kinds of responses he could make if he were "only human."

As Jesus, looking into the face of Martha and seeing her fatigue and irritation, your heart goes out to her. On the other hand, when you look back into the face of Mary, you see her embarrassment and shame. Your heart goes out to her. You love them both, don't you?

Jesus loves every part of you. Do you believe this?

Day 5
Luke 10:38-41

Picture the scene as Jesus sits in the middle of a conflict between two sisters. Imagine the one who can turn water into wine and cast out demons stationed between two sisters at odds with each other.

Put yourself in Jesus' place. Feel the pressure to answer in such a way that you will be true to yourself. You long to meet the needs of each sister even more than you want to ease the tension between them.

You take a breath and take a risk. You have to say the right thing, the thing that comes from your heart. You must speak the truth that will set both of these sisters free.

Stand up and place your hands on Martha's arms. Reach up and soothe her troubled brow with your strong hand. Hear your quiet, but firm chiding of Martha. See the expression on her face as you teach her about putting first things first.

You don't want to embarrass her or shame her. You don't want to discount her fine sense of responsibility, but you do want her to know that there really is only one important thing, and that is loving you. You want her to know that all of the acts of service she can do are for naught if she doesn't love you. How does Martha look at you? What does she do? What does she say?

What would the Living Christ say to your overresponsible self?

Day 6

Luke 10:38-41

Begin today's meditation by creating a mental picture of the scene in this passage. Hear the words of Jesus to Martha. Now picture yourself as Jesus, turning from Martha and sitting down again with Mary still beside your chair. All is quiet in the room; it's sort of an embarrassed silence. You know that it is up to you to shape the direction of the conversation.

You want to affirm Mary's choice to spend time with you. You know that others do not understand. You realize that it is even a break in custom for her to sit in the room with you and the other men, learning from you as if she were a man.

When you look at Mary, you know that she doesn't feel she has to earn your approval or love by working hard or doing enough good deeds for you. She is able to receive and give love without clouding the issue with righteous deeds and good works. This is a woman who understands what it means to be in close, personal, intimate relationship with you, the Lord of life.

When you observe Mary, you know that she wants to be with you just for the sake of being with you. She isn't trying to get anything from you. She isn't spending time with you so that you will do something for her. She isn't trying to earn any points with you. Mary just loves spending time with you.

Do you want to be with Jesus just because you love him?

Day 7
Luke 10:38-41

Imagine yourself as Jesus again, sitting with Mary. You still hear the clatter of dishes. You feel intense hunger pangs as you smell the sweet aromas of meal preparation. Your mouth waters as you see the food being placed on the low table in the other room, and your heart goes out in gratitude to Martha.

You look deep into Mary's eyes again, knowing that what your father wants for all of His followers is that kind of devotion and purity of heart and mind. If only all your disciples had the courage simply to sit with you and love you.

You look at Mary and assess her response to what has happened. Does she feel exonerated? Is she embarrassed at being scolded in front of the others and especially in front of you? Will she pay later for her devotion to you?

You know that she has chosen the best thing by staying with you and loving you, but you also know the value of fulfilling responsibility. You must teach Mary this value. You must let her know that spending time with you does not exempt her from the responsibilities of the home. Communion with you is not an excuse for escaping real life chores.

What is it like for you to have to teach balance to your disciples? How do you help people learn to put first things first? Do you wonder if your disciples will ever understand?

Is there some lesson the Living Christ wants to teach you? Do you spend enough time with him to know what he wants?

KNOW MY INITIATIVE

From the beginning, God the Father took the initiative to come to His children. Even in the Garden of Eden, God sought out Adam and Eve to inquire about their whereabouts.

God initiated dialogue with the great heroes throughout biblical history, often inviting them to join with Him in carrying out some great act on behalf of others. The protecting, providing God watched over the children of Israel. God acted to free them from slavery, care for them as they made their journey through the wilderness, and took the initiative to meet their needs.

God took on human form in the person of Jesus, choosing to identify with human beings to the fullest extent possible. While many people approached Jesus when he was on earth, God the Son took the initiative to walk into people's lives to heal them, teach them, and confront them with the possibility of abundant life. God initiated, through Jesus, the act of redemption.

Before his death Jesus promised the disciples that he would come to them in another way and in another form. Even today, through the power of the Holy Spirit, the Living Christ comes to us to comfort, teach, and guide us toward wholeness.

As you explore the various ways Jesus took the initiative in individual lives while he was on earth, open your heart and mind to the countless ways he is initiating conversation with you even now. Remember that even the impulse to seek him is a result of the fact that he has found you. Even your thought to pray is your response to his praying to you.

HONORING DOUBT

Appearing to the Disciples

John 20:19-29

Day 1
John 20:19-23

Drawing on all your powers of imagination and calling on the inspiration of the Holy Spirit, place yourself in the position of the Resurrected Christ as he stands outside the room where the disciples are huddled together after the crucifixion.

Feel the wood of the door against your hands. Look over your shoulder and notice a guard who cannot see you. Listen to the muffled sounds coming from the room. Someone tells another to lower his voice. You hear weeping.

You have put these friends through great anguish. You are aware that they are confused because what they had expected from you did not come to pass. Your heart aches when you think they had to see you hanging naked on a criminal's cross.

You breathe deeply and turn your attention to the Father's voice. Connected perfectly to Him, you listen for His instructions. When He is ready, you move through the door and stand in the room with the disciples.

Look at their faces when they see you. Notice the shock and surprise on Matthew's face. Feel the warmth of the embrace when John hugs you. Feel the firm handshake of Andrew.

"Peace be with you," you tell them, and then you let them see the wounds in your hands and on your side. "Where is Thomas?" you ask, even though you already know.

Sometimes the Resurrected Christ comes to us in ways we don't expect. Where might he be for you today?

Day 2
John 20:19-21

As Jesus, return to that small room. Sit down with the disciples. They move so they can be close to you. Hear one of them ask a servant to bring you something to eat and drink. How little they understand your nature now!

Candlelight flickers on the faces of the disciples. One of them goes over to make sure the door is still locked. They struggle to understand that you are no longer constrained by doors and locks.

Watch the love in their eyes as you communicate what it means to have moved beyond the grave to this glorious, resurrected state. Remind them of the things you told them before you died. Tell them again about the Advocate who is to come.

The disciples strain to understand who you are now. You assure them that you are the same, but that you are no longer limited by flesh. Some accept what you say; others question you more closely.

Feel the Father's love for each dear friend enter into your being. The unconditional love flows from God, through you, and into their lives. You emanate mercy and grace. You are the conduit through which forgiveness flows. As the disciples receive the gift of your mercy, you remind them that their task is to extend the love of the Father into a broken and dying world.

Practice seeing yourself as the conduit through which all the goodness of God flows freely out into the lives of others. Is your heart open to the presence of the Resurrected Christ?

Day 3
John 20:24-29

Return, with the creative gift of imagination, to that same doorway. Picture yourself as Jesus a week after your first meeting with the disciples.

Stand outside the door and hear the voice of Thomas. Note the anguish in his voice as he declares his refusal to believe unless he sees and touches the actual wounds in your hands and side. You smile to yourself. One of the reasons you chose Thomas as a disciple was because of his independence. No one can own his mind.

Your heart fills with love as you hear the disciples telling about their experience with you a week ago. You know that their lives have changed and their faith has been strengthened because of your presence with them, but Thomas wants to draw his own conclusions. You remember how important it was for you to have a disciple who would not be easily influenced by others.

Again you feel the rough wood of the door against your hands. The same guard stands on alert, but he cannot see you. Walk into the room and observe the disciples.

Suddenly Thomas looks up and recognizes you. His eyes widen in astonishment, and he catches his breath. The room is filled with a silence that wraps you together in power and energy.

"Thomas," you say to him.

Thomas takes a step toward you.

Locked doors and barred windows are nothing for you now; the closed hearts and frozen minds are the most trouble.

What barrier stands between you and the Living Christ?

Day 4

John 20:24-29

Today picture yourself as Jesus standing face to face with Thomas. Say to him, "Peace be with you."

Raise your hands with your wounded palms turned up so that Thomas can see the nailprints. Hear the gasps as you reveal those ugly marks. The movement of your arms causes the roughness of your clothing to brush across the wounds in your side.

You are aware of the other disciples, but you are intensely focused on Thomas. You understand his need to see proof before he can believe. You wanted Thomas for a disciple because of his searching mind. You saw early on that he was an honest seeker and not a proud cynic or an arrogant skeptic.

Thomas lowers his eyes to your hands and flinches. His jaw tightens. A flush covers his face. Beads of sweat pop out across his forehead. You wait while he takes in your torn flesh. Your arms throb as you hold them there, allowing him to take all the time he needs to put his thoughts together. As you watch him, your heart nearly breaks with longing for him to be released from the chains of his logical thinking. You want him to accept you for who you are and for what you want to do in his life. "You can touch me, Thomas," you tell him.

Watch Thomas as he stares at your wounds. You love him through those difficult moments as his mind makes the transition from doubt to recognition. You give Thomas exactly what he needs in order to make his leap of faith.

Can you give up reason to accept mystery? Can you give up logic to receive grace?

Day 5
John 20:24-29

Using your abilities to create mental pictures, return to the scene in the closed room at the moment when the eyes of Thomas are drawn to the wounded hands of Jesus.

See yourself as Jesus in that moment. Feel the tension in the room as the disciples stand around the two of you. All the attention is focused on what transpires between you and Thomas.

Feel the throbbing pain shoot up and down your arms as you wait for Thomas. You open your hands to him; the wounds in your hands sting as the flesh pulls. You wait patiently.

Once again Thomas slowly raises his eyes to yours. You nod slightly, and he begins to lift one hand to yours. Gently he places one finger on the edge of your palm. He lifts his other hand and tentatively places it on your other hand, palm to palm, and you feel a shudder ripple through his body.

The two of you stand silently with your palms touching. It is as if Thomas wants to impress exactly how each wound feels upon each of his own hands and mind.

Thomas removes his hands. You tell him that he can reach out and touch the wounds in your side. Hesitantly, he reaches for you, and when he connects with your woundedness, a convulsive sob thunders from his heart and through his throat.

"Stop doubting, Thomas," you tell him. "You have the proof you need in these wounds. Believe, Thomas; believe."

Who is the wounded healer in your life? How are you a wounded healer? How does the Great Physician work to heal you?

Day 6
John 20:24-29

Re-create the powerful moment when the intellectual doubts of Thomas evaporate. Imagine yourself as Jesus, standing there with Thomas as he makes a leap of faith from doubt to certainty. Watch the shift in Thomas' body as his thoughts shift from questioning to knowing.

Imagine how Jesus feels when he hears Thomas' affirmation of belief. Feel the joy flood through Jesus when Thomas declares his faith. See the delight in Jesus as Thomas moves out of the darkness of confusion and into the light of clarity.

As Jesus, hear Thomas say, "My Lord and my God!" Experience the pleasure of connectedness with one of your dearest friends. You are known for who you are, and that gives great relief.

Watch Jesus respond to Thomas in a way that is consistent with Thomas' temperament.

Sensing that Thomas does not need an emotional display at this point as much as he needs to move back into intellectual understanding, Jesus speaks a clear, concise word of truth to Thomas. Knowing that he doesn't need a long philosophical explanation, Jesus gets straight to the point. He must also know that Thomas will be sensing the eyes of the other disciples on him.

Recall a moment when you made a leap from doubt to faith, from questioning to assurance, from fear to faith. Thank the Risen Christ for meeting you at the point of your need. How are you different because of your belief?

Day 7

John 20:24-29

As Jesus, put yourself back in the room with the disciples. You sense the slight movements of the disciples and know that they don't want to break the mood of the moment.

You have accomplished what you came to do and are satisfied that your work with Thomas, at least for this phase of his spiritual journey, is completed.

As Thomas looks into your eyes, you see a changed face. The eyes that look at you now are those of a child, trusting and open. The face, once hard and cold, is now relaxed.

Hear yourself tell Thomas that he is blessed because his doubt has been met with proof. Watch his expression become more serious as you make your next point.

"Others will believe who have never seen what you have been privileged to see, Thomas," you say.

The other disciples begin to whisper among themselves. You want Thomas to know that some will believe only because they will hear his story.

Your heart aches because you know that not every believer will have the privilege of visual proof. As you look around the room and into the faces of each disciple, you know that you can entrust your love and message of redemption to each one.

In Thomas, though, you see that the man before you is transformed. He will have answers that are better than any logical reasons or rational wonderings can provide him. Now Thomas has the answer of the heart.

Will you allow the Living Christ to transform your heart?

SECOND CHANCES
Reinstating Peter

John 21:1-19

Day 1

John 21:1-6

Imagine a scene by the Sea of Tiberius in the cool of morning just before dawn. Put yourself in that scene, standing on the shore. Hear the lapping of the water against the land. See the vegetation along the shoreline and the fishermen out in their boats. Smell the early morning scents of water and earth.

You watch your disciples, who have returned to their old jobs. Now and then one of the fishermen glances at you, but none of them recognize you. How does it feel? Do you want it that way?

You breathe deeply, connected even more intimately now with your heavenly father. Your actions are intentional, guided by the will of God. You know exactly what you are doing and why you are doing it. You are completely in charge of this situation.

At the right time you call out to the fishermen. Hear your voice as you ask them about their catch. You always meet folks where they are, don't you?

Hear yourself call out advice from the shore. You wait to see if they will follow guidance from the shore. Watch with joy as the disciples follow your guidance and bring in a big catch.

As you go about your work today, imagine Jesus watching you. What advice might he give you about your work?

Day 2
John 21:1-7

As if you were an artist, re-create the scene from this passage. Make the picture in your mind's eye sensory-rich; experience it with all your physical senses. See the sights. Hear the sounds. Smell the aromas. Taste the sea breeze. Feel the cool morning breeze on your face.

Step into the scene as Jesus, preparing for a glad reunion with your beloved friends. You know that they have been changed by the crucifixion.

Your own heart skips a beat when you hear John say to Peter, "It is the Lord!" The last time you and Peter saw each other was in the courtyard when he betrayed you not once, but three times. How will he respond? Will he be glad to see you?

True to form, impulsive, impestuous Peter jumps out of the boat and rushes toward you, leaving the other fishermen to haul in the biggest catch of their lives.

Watch Peter as he hurries to you. See the ecstasy and jubilation in his face when he makes eye contact with you. Are those tears of relief and gladness? You hold out your arms and shout the name of this man you love, this disciple who betrayed you.

You see questions in his face. You know that he wonders if he can ever make things right with you, if you can ever forgive him. He probably wonders how you got there.

When has the Living Christ come back to you after you left him?

Day 3
John 21:1-14

On this day put yourself in Jesus' place as he prepares a picnic on the beach. See him building the fire and tending it while the disciples contend with their huge catch of fish.

You cook the fish and prepare the bread. Once again you use simple things such as loaves and fish to show who you are and how you want to relate to others. You are about the business of drawing people to God, especially these people.

You sit down on the ground beside the fire and watch it leap and dance in the morning air. Fill your lungs with the smells of water and fish. Break off a piece of bread and eat it, giving thanks for the provision. Look out into the distance and celebrate the dawning of a new day. Savor the sunrise and relish the sounds of your friends as they pull in their catch and contend with the reality of your appearance.

One by one the disciples join you. Some bring the best fish from the catch, and you cook it for them. You know that they are hungry, but you also sense they are bursting with excitement, wanting to know what you are doing here with them.

They don't dare ask you, and you wait for the right time to quench their curiosity. You serve them their breakfast. You, Incarnate God, accommodate yourself to human need in such a way.

Make a list of the ways the Living Christ has met your needs. Be awestruck at the ways he has accommodated himself to you. What need might he want to meet today?

Day 4
John 21:1-15

Enter the scene by the side of the lake at the moment when the hunger pangs have been quieted by the breakfast Jesus has prepared. In your mind's eye sit back with Jesus and live the moment when the frenzy of the big catch and the hurry to eat have subsided.

The big questions about who you are, where you have been, and how things will be now hang unspoken in the air between you and the disciples. Out of reverence and awe, the disciples wait for you to speak. Perhaps they are a bit afraid. Most likely they are hurt and confused; after all, they had to go back home and explain to their families how you ended up on a criminal's cross. You feel deep sorrow for putting them through that ordeal.

You know that Peter must be feeling nervous. Surely he must wonder if you are going to settle a score with him. He must be afraid that you might censure him or banish him from your work. You turn your eyes to Peter, and he immediately meets your gaze. He searches your face, trying to read you.

Quietly, you ask him if he loves you more than these. You want to hear Peter say that he loves you more than anything else in his life—more than catching fish, more than any other human being, more than his reputation, more than anything. Feel your heart soar as Peter answers, "Yes, Lord, I love you."

What do you love more than Jesus?

Day 5
John 21:1-17

Using your imagination, feel the intensity of the moment when Jesus asks Peter the most significant question of the fisherman's life. Watch as both men deal with strong emotion. Feel with the heart of Jesus the longing for restoration and reconciliation. Imagine yourself searching Peter's face for any wavering in commitment to you. Look deep into his eyes to see if there is any faltering.

You know that Peter has punished himself enough for his betrayal of you. Whatever you could do to censure or punish him would be nothing compared to the agony he has inflicted upon himself.

With the wisdom the Heavenly Father gives you, however, you know that Peter needs to clarify for himself where he stands with you. How things are between the two of you isn't nearly as important for you to know as it is for Peter. You want to know if Peter loves you, but the real need is for Peter to declare it.

So you ask him again, "Do you truly love me?" He tells you he does, and you tell him he must take care of your people. To drive the point home, though, you ask him one more time. See the frustration and hurt on Peter's face. Hear his answer. Feel the peace in your heart when you hear his profession of love.

What if Jesus insisted on knowing where he stands with you?

Day 6

John 21:1-19

Imagine how it would feel to have the wisdom and sensitivity of Jesus so that you know just how far to push when dealing with strong, impetuous types like Peter. How would it feel to have such perception and wisdom that you know exactly the right questions to ask of your followers?

What difference would it make to you to be so closely aligned with God and have such highly developed intuition and reason that you are able to interact with individuals with the same effectiveness Jesus did?

Put yourself in Jesus' place in the moment when he knows for certain that Peter loves him and is committed to him. Imagine knowing that your questions have peeled away all the layers of Peter's defenses so that he, too, is convinced about how he stands with you. As much as you are able, imagine the power and peace of being connected with God and another human being at the same time.

How would it be to be Jesus and commission Peter? How would it be to entrust this fisherman with the task of feeding your sheep, tending your lambs, and being a major player in establishing an amazing, revolutionary new enterprise?

You look in Peter's face and wonder if he knows what you are asking of him. You believe in this man. You know that he is teachable and leadable and can be trusted to carry on your work.

Can the Living Christ trust you with his work?

Day 7

John 21

Picturing yourself as Jesus, stand up and motion for Peter to follow you away from the fire where the other disciples sit.

Peter stands up, and you begin walking along the shoreline. You want to tell him more about what it means to tend your lambs and feed your sheep. You want to explain what is to come and what part he will play in the magnificent unfolding of God's plan for redemption in the world.

You glance behind you and see that John is following the two of you. Peter looks, too, and asks you, "What about him?"

You smile patiently. Peter still has a way to go before he reaches the maturity he needs.

You walk a few paces and let Peter hear his questions echoing in the silence.

"I'll take care of John," you tell him. "John isn't your business. You've got to decide if you are going to follow me or not."

Let your words confront Peter. Let him recognize that his business is to stay focused on where the two of you stand with each other.

"You've got to mind your own business," you tell him.

"But what about tending lambs and feeding sheep?" he asks you. "How do I mind my own business and do that?"

"You'll learn," you tell him. "It's about priorities."

According to Jesus, what is your business? What is not?

WALKING ON WATER

Calming Seas and Hearts

Matthew 14:22-33
Mark 6:45-61

Day 1
Matthew 14:22-33; Mark 6:45-61

Walk with Jesus and the disciples beside the Sea of Galilee. The sun is setting. You watch fishermen, gathering their nets and their catch, getting ready to go home to their families.

You and the disciples have just experienced something grand and glorious with the feeding of the multitudes, and you all feel the exhilaration of that experience. How amazing it is to be a part of God's miraculous activity, released through you, his Son. How wonderful to share his provision in such a way that it meets human need and manifests God's glory at the same time. You hope that everyone knows the source of your power. You pray that the disciples, especially, will connect all the dots.

The day has depleted your energy, however, and you yearn for the necessary solitude with your father. You send the disciples ahead of you by boat and make your way up into the familiar hills. You can hardly wait to be alone with God, to talk over the events of the day, to receive His guidance and instruction, and simply to rest in His presence. Communion with the Father is as necessary to you as eating and drinking are to your physical body.

You walk steadfastly to a place where you can be alone. You sit down and look out across the lake. Here and there a star appears in the sky. You rest in union with God.

After a big event, communion with God is necessary. Do you take it? Are you disciplined about spending time alone with God?

Day 2
Matthew 14:22-33

Return with Jesus to the place of solitude in the hills surrounding the Sea of Galilee. See him resting, perhaps leaning against a strong, sturdy tree. Feel the cool night air. Hear the rustle of the wind as a storm begins to brew.

Imagine Jesus as he becomes aware of the storm. Watch him stand up and scan the lake. He knows that his disciples are out on the tempestuous lake, and his concern for them increases as the storm grows in intensity.

With Jesus, walk down the mountainside toward the lake. Your eyes are on the disciples. You sense their fear and distress, so you pick up your speed to get to them a little faster. Your own fatigue gives way to concern for your dearest friends.

Ever connected to your heavenly father, you turn within to your heart and ask Him for help. As naturally as breathing, united with the power of your father, you begin to walk across the water. God the Father, sovereign over all of nature, fills you with all that is necessary to meet the needs of your disciples, and you cooperate fully with Him. Ever surrendered to his divine purpose and energy, you make yourself God's instrument right there on the Sea of Galilee. You and the sea obey God's will. You and the sea belong to Him. Right now, your disciples are in trouble; quickly, you draw near to them.

Imagine how your life would be different if you were totally surrendered to the will of Almighty God. What cost is there to that kind of surrender?

Day 3
Matthew 14:22-33

Pick up the storm scene in your imaginative prayer. See the disciples, tossed about in a small boat on raging water. Hear the sounds of their voices, frightened and confused. Smell the rain; feel it beating on your face as you walk across the water. Taste the water on your lips. Feel the cold wind.

As you walk, however, your awareness of the intense fear of the disciples takes center stage. When you hear the terror in their voices, it breaks your heart. Don't they know that you are there, nearer than they can imagine?

When you watch them flailing around, trying to secure the ropes and steady the boat, you feel their panic. You don't want your followers to experience this kind of fear. You want them to be able to go through storms—literal and figurative—with the serenity they need.

You must teach them that fear distorts thinking processes and clouds judgment. You must help them to have the assurance that no matter what they are going through in the outside world, their inner world can be calm and quiet. They can always stay connected to the Father and His saving power.

You move closer to the boat, step by step on the water. Can't they see that you are drawing near to them? Why don't they take their focus off the storm long enough to look up? Can't they sense your presence? Is fear really so strong in them that it keeps them from knowing you are right there?

How good are you at letting God guide you moment by moment?

Day 4
Matthew 14:22-33

On this day join the drama on the raging sea in the moment when the disciples spy Jesus walking on the water toward them. As Jesus, hear their terror escalate when they see you. Watch them try to save themselves. Hear their shouts for help.

How often you appear, only to be mistaken for something or someone else. How often your followers don't recognize you when you come to help. If they weren't so scared, you could be amused because they mistake you for a ghost. You mustn't laugh, though; after all, they can't help it if they can't see the big picture. Fully confident, you smile to yourself.

You must help the disciples understand that you are always present, even in the midst of their difficulties. You must teach them that fear is the opposite of love and that fear makes them think you aren't present. You must inform them that fear often causes misperceptions and makes folks unable to see clearly. You are the corrective lens for that vision problem.

Getting closer to them, you walk confidently as the wind and rain whip around you. You could stop the storm immediately, but you see a higher purpose in this event. Sometimes fear sharpens the awareness of need for you. At times fear is the one thing that will make people cry out for you. There are moments when it is only fear that makes proud and able people come to the awareness of how much they need your power and presence.

What difference does it make to know that the Living Christ is always present, always watching, in the storms of your life?

Day 5

Matthew 14:22-33

Imagine yourself as Jesus on this day, walking across water toward your disciples. Experience the high drama of the raging sea, the terrified disciples, and the steady, guiding hand of your heavenly father who is always with you. See the sights. Hear the sounds. Feel the heartbeat of Jesus as he heads across the water to help his friends.

Hear your strong voice call out to them, identifying yourself. "Take courage!" you tell them. You intend to calm the storm, but right now it is more important that you calm the disciples within the storm.

Hear Peter call out to you. Hear him throw out a challenge. Hear your voice as you counter with your own challenge to his faith and fortitude.

Watch Peter climb over the side of the boat. Hold your breath as he starts out, walking across the water to you. His eyes are locked with yours. You and he are connected in a way Peter has never experienced before.

Feel your heart sink when you see Peter take his eyes off you and glance up at the rain. In that instant of disconnecting from you, he loses heart and allows fear to take over his will and mind. You watch him sink instantly and hear him scream for you to help him. Your power went out of him the minute he gave in to his fear. Just as quickly, you reach out your strong hand and catch Peter just before he goes under.

What would "walking on water" be for you right now?

Day 6

Matthew 14:22-33

Reenter the scene on the water in the moment when Jesus reaches out for Peter and saves him. As Jesus, you are aware of the disciples in the boat, watching the encounter between you and Peter. You see their shocked faces. You hear their disbelief as they mutter to each other about impulsive, impestuous Peter.

You look into Peter's face. Is he embarrassed? Humiliated? Ashamed of himself? Is he more bothered that he tested you and himself on the water or that he took his eyes off you? Which will he remember: the fact that he had the courage to take the leap toward you or that, in fear, he waffled. Will he remember the ecstasy of being fully connected with you, or will he focus on the moment when he sank?

You look into his eyes and long for him to remember the moment when he was empowered by your presence. You hope that he will think about it, ponder it, and reach for it again.

The two of you look at each other. You don't scold him for his lack of faith. You don't shame him for trying. You don't send him away because he couldn't follow through with his endeavor. You are simply with him, moving him with you toward the boat.

You know Peter's frailties. You are fully aware of his rough edges, those places in him where his faith runs out and his fear takes over. Still, you see in him untapped power and energy. You also know his humility and love him very much.

When the Living Christ looks into your heart, what does he see?

Day 7
Matthew 14:22-33

With the heart of Jesus, imagine yourself climbing into the boat on the storm-tossed sea. Picture yourself joining the disciples in their little boat, wet and bedraggled from the wind and rain.

In the instant you join them in the boat, you speak the word, "Peace, be still." Immediately the wind dies down, the waters stop rolling, and a calm pervades the disciples' minds and hearts. In your presence all things become quiet and still. With you, there is peace.

Watch the disciples' looks of amazement. Sense their bodies relax and their spirits settle down as they experience the full impact of your power and presence. Live in the "calm after the storm," the moment when all is well.

One by one, the disciples turn to look into your eyes. You think that one of them might ask you what took you so long to get to them. You wonder if someone will ask why you let them get into the storm in the first place.

What you see in their eyes, however, is pure love for you. They see you for who you are, and they worship you. The power you have demonstrated that came directly from your father through you to them has touched them deeply. They believe as never before that you are who you say you are. You are the Son of God.

When storms rage without and within, will you allow the Living Christ to "climb into your boat" and bring his peace?

DO YOU WANT TO
GET WELL?

Healing the Man at Bethesda's Pool

John 5:1-15

Day 1

John 5:1-15

Picture Jesus moving from place to place in Jerusalem, making the most of the holy days and feast days. See him entering into the festivities and observances of his people.

Watch him enjoy being out and about with persons from all walks of life. Notice how he is always seeking out those who need him. Always he makes his choices under God's guidance.

On this day visualize yourself as Jesus going to the Sheep Gate, or Bethesda, a pool surrounded by five alcoves. As you walk out of the street and into this area, your eyes are bombarded by the multitude of sick and disabled people. In various stages of illness and infirmity, they lie or sit on the ground and lean against the building. You take it all in—the blind, the crippled, and the paralyzed.

Why are they like this, you wonder? And why are there so many of them? Do you wonder why God has allowed so much suffering? Even more troubling for you is knowing whose need to meet and which one to meet first. Where do you start? You listen for the Father's voice.

You know that the waters stir periodically. It is rumored that an angel stirs the water and that those who can get to the water can be healed.

Make a list of all of the places where you could expend your energy and exercise your unique gifts. What is top priority?

Day 2
John 5:1-15

Move back into the meditation from this story in the Gospels at the point where Jesus is standing in one of the alcoves of the pool at Bethesda. Ask God the Father to help you open your mind and heart to think and feel in the same manner as Jesus.

As you scan the crowd, one of the invalids, a man, catches your attention. You have seen him there before. You know that he has been lying by the pool for thirty-eight years. You shake your head in disbelief.

Compelled by the guiding touch of your father, you walk slowly toward this man. With the perception that comes from your unique intimacy with God, you are able to see beneath the obvious problem—the man's infirmity—to the soul issue. You notice that healing needs to take place at more than one level, and you rise to the challenge of meeting this man where he is.

"Do you want to get well?" you ask the man, as soon as you are near enough for him to look you in the eye.

What kind of question is that? The man looks at you in disbelief. Is he insulted? Does he think you have lost your mind? If you had been in his place, lying there for thirty-eight years, you wouldn't have had to ask such a ridiculous question.

You see it all in the man's eyes. You continue to gaze right into his eyes. It is as if you can see all the way to his soul.

To what have you been hanging onto for a very long time?

Day 3

John 5:1-15

Enter today's meditation at the moment when Jesus stands eye to eye with the longtime invalid. Imagine what is going through Jesus' mind after he asks his outrageous question. Never forget that he designs each healing to fit the individual need. If he had been talking to this man's neighbor, he would have used a different approach, an approach to meet his need.

As Jesus, you hear the man begin to tell you the reasons why he has been there so long, unhealed. Hear him make excuses. Listen to his blaming of others. Wait patiently while he goes through his litany of justification.

You stand, a pillar of strength and majesty. You don't buy what the man is selling. You know that it has become his habit to blame forces outside himself for his condition. You realize that this man has a much bigger problem than his weakened body—his attitude.

You don't accept his excuses, but neither do you insult or demean him. You know that it is often easy to get trapped in weakness, sickness, helplessness, or hopelessness. While you know that not all people use infirmity as a crutch, you also know how illness can become a habit, a place to hide, a good excuse for not becoming all you can be.

Is there anyone in your life to whom you would like to ask this question? What if you asked it about yourself?

Day 4
John 5:1-15

Begin today by placing yourself, in your imagination, beside the pool of Bethseda. Hear the voices of the infirm. See them rush to the water when it stirs. Notice a relative helping his loved one get to the water.

You are standing face to face with a man whom you have challenged. You have heard his excuses, and you know that, as in all excuses, there may be an element of truth in what he says. You also know that if you need an excuse, any will do.

Looking deep into the man's eyes, you move past all of the layers of excuses and rationalizations. You move even deeper through more layers of pain and regret, feelings of failure and remorse for wasted years and lost opportunities. You touch a part of this man that used to be able to hope. You connect with his shame and guilt, his anger and rage, listening always for the guidance of your father.

You know what the man needs. You connect with what strength there is in his will. You touch the part of him that still believes and wants to be whole and healthy.

Hear your voice command him to stand up, pick up his bedroll, and start walking. Hear the strength and virility in your tone.

Watch the man's expression as he thinks over what you have commanded him to do. Notice the incredible moment when the healing power of your father, flowing through you, touches the man's soul and turns on the light in his eyes.

What part of you needs a strong command from the Lord?

Day 5

John 5:1-15

Begin today's meditation by imagining you are Jesus, looking into the face of the man by the pool. You have commanded him to get up and walk.

Focused on the decision-making process with this man as his lame self and his healthy self carry on a dialogue with each other, you are also aware of what is going on around you. In the immediate vicinity there is a holy hush. It is as if the people close by are acutely aware that something important is happening. On the other hand, perhaps they are still mulling over your question: "Do you want to get well?"

You hear some whispers beyond the area where you are engaged in a life-changing encounter with this man. Further out, life goes on as usual. How many times, you wonder, is your father carrying out some amazing event while the rest of the world does not notice.

Still, you gaze into the man's eyes. You sense the very moment when he makes his decision. Watch him look around and then look back at you.

Does he wonder for a minute how things will be different if he is whole and well and responsible? Does he question whether he can learn how to walk, work, and make his way in the world? Does he have any remorse about leaving his long-time friends behind? Or does this man seize the moment of God's grace with complete abandonment to His mercy and love?

What is it like to let go of self-defeating thoughts and ways?

Day 6
John 5:1-15

Adapting the process to every situation, Jesus knew exactly how much to do for people. He always moved in to meet them with his power and adequacy and do for them what they could not do for themselves. On the other hand, he never did for people what they needed to do for themselves. Now and then he asked people to cooperate in their own healing and participate in their own wellness program. In this story he asked the man to stand up, carry his own pallet, and walk.

Imagine yourself as Jesus, watching the man struggle to his feet. Get in touch with Jesus' heart as he sees the man try out his legs. Feel the lump in your throat when the man, standing straight and proud, does, in fact, pick up his own pallet and begin to walk.

What is in your heart, Jesus, when you heal someone like this? What is it like for you when someone triumphs over difficulty and overcomes seemingly unmovable obstacles? How do you feel when one of your loved ones is victorious in managing a ravaging character defect?

What does it do to you when you know that you have been the one to set a prisoner free, open blind eyes and hearts and minds, and put people on the course to freedom and mercy and grace? How do you like being the instrument through which God makes people whole?

What is it in a person that frees the Living Christ to bring about the wholeness and salvation he wants for everyone?

Day 7
John 5:1-15

Fast-forward the scene in today's reading to some time after the dramatic healing by the pool. Join Jesus in the Temple area. Walk with him among the people. Imagine yourself as Jesus watching the man you healed. You know that the religious authorities have been talking about the incident; the fact that you performed this healing miracle on the Sabbath has become a point of contention among the authorities.

What would you have felt when you saw the man? How would you have responded, if you had been Jesus, when the man came up to thank you for what you had done for him? Would you prefer that he not call attention to you? Would you like it if you could speak with him in a more private place?

Hear your voice greeting the man. See the delight in his eyes as he looks into yours. Something in you sounds an alarm of caution, however. Is it your father? Is this a warning?

You caution the man about returning to his old ways. You know that just as he participated in his healing, he can also drift back to his old ways. For this particular man and his infirmity, eternal vigilance is going to be the price of his freedom. For this man, lifestyle choices are crucial; they are also within his control.

Will this man stay well? Will he stay whole and sane? Will he have the humility to follow your guidance?

Wanting to be well and staying well are two separate issues. People are slaves because freedom is hard and slavery is easy. Which do you prefer: slavery or freedom?

KNOW MY LOVE

For God so loved the world that he gave his only begotten son that whosoever believes in him would not perish, but would have eternal life. (John 3:16)

The life of Jesus was one of love. One can see the very essence of who he was in his loving acts that took place while he walked the hills and valleys of a specific place at a specific time in history.

This was a man who loved nature. He used the birds of the air and flowers of the field as visual aids, holding them up as teaching tools.

Jesus loved family and community life. He loved his friends and family. Note the compassion and tenderness with which he held little children and took care of his mother. Read the Gospels and see how much time he spent with his disciples. Jesus loved the whole world, and he loved individual persons.

Jesus loved the Scriptures and the law, religious practices and observances. But more than all these, he loved his heavenly father and the new life his father wanted him to convey to his followers. This new life had to do with love; it was formed in love and is about love.

Always the Son of Man extended love. He initiated relationships with others out of love. Jesus gave love lavishly and freely. Today, through the power of the Holy Spirit, Jesus the Christ extends his love to you.

SEEING THE LIGHT
Healing Blindness

John 9:1-41

Day 1

John 9:1-2

Imagine yourself as Jesus, trying to explain the new wine of your father's kingdom to people who are programmed to see things in the old way.

Remember a time when you were trying to convince people whose minds were locked in to the past to consider doing things a new way. Remember your frustration when you kept running up against the stone wall of another's defenses; no matter how hard you tried, they wouldn't let in the fresh breezes of the spirit.

Picture yourself, then, as Jesus, wanting to impart simple but profound truths to set people free, only to be misunderstood and misquoted.

Put yourself in Jesus' shoes, walking along a village street with your disciples. One of them sees a blind man and asks you to explain his blindness.

As you look at your disciples, you know that the way of the world is always to find someone to blame. You know about cause and effect, but you also know that blaming someone for their physical difficulties isn't the answer. In fact, blaming always leads to dead ends. You know, too, that spiritual blindness is the worst blindness of all.

What new truth might the Living Christ want you to see today? Is it possible that you are spiritually blind?

240

Day 2
John 9:1-4

Imagine yourself as Jesus with the deep longing in your heart for your disciples to take their focus off their problem and place it on God your father? You know that continuing to analyze the problem or finding someone to blame for the problem will not solve it. How can you illustrate the awesome power of God so that the disciples will be healed of their own spiritual blindness?

As Jesus, you make it look so easy. You take such ordinary elements and breathe your holy breath into them. You do such simple deeds that have profound and life-altering effects.

Imagine yourself as Jesus. Look at the face of the blind man standing before you. Your heart wrenches when you look into his eyes that cannot see you. Your heart aches when you hear even your disciples talking about the man as if he cannot hear. You want to weep when you think about all the sunsets, flowers, and friends' faces he has never seen.

Even more, you are filled with anguish when you realize the curse this man has lived under; he takes the blame for being born blind. You sense his shame as he stands there with you, so vulnerable and dependent on others.

Your heart sinks even further, though, when you realize that curing this man's blindness is simple compared to healing the spiritual blindness of people whose hearts are cold and hard and whose minds are set.

If Jesus were to heal your life, where would he start?

Day 3
John 9:1-7

Reenter the scene in this week's passage by creating a visual picture of Jesus standing with the blind men. See their clothes and sandals. Notice the way disciples are gathered around them.

Now imagine yourself as Jesus. Feel the breeze on your face and the solid earth beneath your feet. Children's laughter and sounds of the marketplace form the background noise.

With the heart of Jesus, feel the compassion for this blind man. Stoop down, spit in the dust, and make a paste with your saliva in the palm of your hand.

See the paste form in your hand. Notice the color of it, a color this man cannot see. Feel the texture change as basic elements merge with each other. Think about what can happen when your divine nature merges with the heart, mind, and will of others. Ponder the profound changes that occur when your father's will merges with yours.

All voices around you have become eerily quiet. All eyes are focused on you. You are connected to your father. There are no barriers between you. You know that it is His will for this man to see, and the way He is going to accomplish this is through you.

See yourself as you rub the healing paste on the man's eyes. Hear your voice tell him how to participate in his own healing.

What thing in your life might God want to use to make you see?

Day 4

John 9:1-34

Imagine yourself as Jesus in the moment when you have rubbed the healing paste on the blind man's eyes. You stand there and watch him go toward the pool of Siloam, led by one of your disciples. Your heart soars because you have participated with God, the Great Physician, in an act of mercy on behalf of one of God's children.

Caught up in the splendor of being God's instrument, you stand in awe and reverence at the work of God. Eager to interpret the healing touch of God to the disciples, you turn your attention back to them.

You hear the faint uproar of people as they follow the blind man to the pool. From a distance you witness his ecstasy when he can see and the response it evokes among the people.

Feel your heart sink when you begin to hear about the adverse reaction of those who would put the letter of the law above meeting the needs of human beings. Feel your disappointment when you run up against the spiritual blindness among the religious elite.

How can this be, you wonder? How can it be that God is opening blind eyes, setting people free, and making people whole among the religious leaders, and they do not recognize the activity of God? How can they be so blind to the dazzling work of God, walking among them?

Is it possible that God is at work all around you and within you, but you do not have eyes to see? Pray for sight.

Day 5

John 9:1-35

On this day imagine yourself as Jesus, walking through the streets near the synagogue. Hear one of your disciples call your name. You turn around and see him running to you. His face is twisted with concern.

When he catches up, the two of you begin walking away from the crowd. In a troubled voice he begins to tell you what he has heard about your healing of the blind man. He repeats the gossip he has picked up in the synagogue area.

Hear him tell you how the synagogue officials have harassed the parents of the man, trying to find out who you are and what you are about. Hear the dismay in his voice when he recounts the ways the officials have interrogated the man. Feel the pleasure in your heart when you hear that the man said, "All I know is this: once I was blind, and now I can see."

You stop on the pathway and turn to face this friend of yours. You understand his dilemma. He wants to be loyal to you, but he is disturbed by what is going on and how it affects you—and him.

You place your hands on his shoulders. You look him straight in the eye. Hear yourself tell him that your heavenly father's chief concern is the healing of people and that he wants to heal their spiritual blindness even more than their physical blindness.

Does your relationship with Christ cause you any discomfort with the world in which you travel? Why or why not?

Day 6

John 9:1-35

Stand with Jesus in the marketplace near the synagogue. Hear the town gossip, centered around the blind man you have healed.

You can't believe it! You would think these people would be rejoicing over the restored sight of one of their own. Surely friends and relatives alike would be thrilled that this man can see. How can they not be glad that the one who was blind can now see?

You watch the people come and go. You hear their whispers and conjectures. You watch the man, trying to explain how he can see.

Do you feel disappointed at not being understood? Are you angry that the townspeople won't accept the blind man's healing? Are you frustrated that his religious system prefers him in his old role so that they can stay in theirs? Are you aghast when they throw the man out of the synagogue?

The man's healing doesn't fit into the carefully crafted religious system; you broke the mold. His healing doesn't give them credit; you give it to your father. His sight changes the definitions and the transactions, and now everyone is confused.

Your disciples join you. How will you teach them discernment in this situation? How can you make sure that they understand what the real problem is?

You ask one of the disciples to bring the man to you.

Do you thwart the healing grace of God with logic and law?

Day 7

John 9:1-41

As Jesus, stand again with the man you healed of blindness. This time when you look into his eyes, you see life and light. Notice the twinkle in his eye. Feel the pleasure of the Father at what you have done for him.

The man looks deep into your eyes, searching for meaning and reason in the absurdity of his culture. You have healed his blind eyes; surely you can do something about the treatment he is getting from his own people.

You place both hands on his shoulders. You talk to him and question him. You make yourself known to him. You want this man to know fully and clearly who you are so that he can stand up to the questions, ridicule, and resistance of those who have eyes but cannot see.

You see a flicker of understanding in the man's eyes. You press him further to acknowledge who you are. You stay with him, firmly planted in the Father's love, until you are convinced he has the spiritual sight he needs to handle his new physical sight.

As Jesus, you are the light that exposes and dispels the darkness. You are the light that brightens, the light that inspires, the light that heals and restores whatever is broken.

No matter how controversy rages around you and this man, you honor his faith in you so much that you will stand with him until you are convinced he is sure about who you are.

How does the Light of the World need to illuminate your darkness?

RECEIVING LOVE
Jesus' Feet Anointed by Mary

Luke 7:36-50

Day 1

Luke 7:36

Was this a set-up or what? If you had been Jesus, would you have wondered why you were invited to a Pharisee's house?

Put yourself in Jesus' place, walking through the doorway of the home of this religious leader. Look around and see the beauty of the house. Notice the servants, quietly setting the dinner table.

As you look into the face of your host, you know that he might be inviting you to his home out of a sincere desire to know you better, explore your teachings, and get in touch with the things that touch your heart. This might very well be a sincere truth-seeker.

On the other hand, you may be on trial. Whatever you say or do here may set you up for censure, ridicule, or worse with the religious establishment. You do know that you will be watched carefully.

Always connected with your father, you are able to walk boldly and confidently into this home, knowing that whatever the motivation of your host, you are the same. Regardless of what this Pharisee is up to, you will do and say what you would anywhere. No other human being decides how you will behave or who you are because you follow the directives of your father.

When you are out and about in the world, to what audience are you playing your life? Are you the same wherever you go?

Day 2
Luke 7:36-38

Imagine that you are Jesus and are a guest in the home of one of the influential leaders of the religious establishment. Picture yourself being escorted to the dining table. Imagine yourself sitting down at the place of honor. See the others gather at the table. Hear the polite sounds of guests and your host. Smell the food. See yourself speak to a servant who rushes to get your drink.

Your host seats himself across from you so that the two of you can make eye contact. You watch him, observing the power and influence he has with the people around the table.

From out of the corner of your eye you see a woman coming from the front room, making her way toward the dining room. Servants try to stop her, but she won't be stopped.

She is a small woman, and her covered head is lowered. In her arms she is holding something wrapped in a shawl.

Suddenly the woman reaches the threshold of the dining room and, briefly, glances in your direction. It is Mary!

What is she doing? Why has she come here? Does she know that she is putting herself at risk, showing up in this home at this gathering? Unnoticed, she moves around the edge of the room toward you. How do you feel about her being here?

When you are put in a potentially compromising position, what do you do?

Day 3
Luke 7:36-38

Enter today's scene at the moment Mary reaches the place where Jesus is sitting at the dining table. Re-create in your imagination the sights, sounds, and aromas of the room.

Put yourself in Jesus' position. You are the honored guest in the home of a Pharisee. Already held in suspicion and misunderstood by the religious establishment, you sit with this woman, a prostitute, standing before you.

Quietly Mary kneels before you. See her remove the covering from her head. Watch her hair fall gracefully around her face. Notice the tears coursing down her cheeks. She looks up at you momentarily; her eyes glisten with love for you.

You watch her wipe your feet with her hair. See her remove a flask from the shawl she has carried. Watch her remove the top and pour some of the expensive perfume into her small hand. With tender compassion she anoints your feet—and you let her do it.

You are aware of a hush in the room, a hush filled with meaning. You know that all eyes are on you. Your eyes are on this woman who is willing to risk everything to show her love for you. You watch her, reviewing her history in your mind. You know the pain she has experienced, and your heart is full of love for her and for her willingness to give to you at any cost.

If you had been Jesus, would you have been more concerned about receiving this gift of love or what the others were thinking?

250

Day 4
Luke 7:36-39

With the power of your imagination, place yourself back in Jesus' position, receiving the anointing of love and perfume from Mary.

Inhale deeply and smell the sweet aroma of the perfume. Experience the tenderness in Mary's hands as she massages the perfume into your feet. Feel her tears fall on your feet. Watch her courage and boldness in offering her gift to you.

You are aware of what the men around you must be thinking, and you smile to yourself. You can see the big picture, but they cannot.

You know that they are wondering how Mary knows you. After all, she is the town harlot. The disciples and the rest will want to know why is she so free to approach you, especially in this public gathering. How did she know where you were? And why don't you stop her?

Fully aligned with your father's will, you don't worry about what these men will think of Mary or her action. You know who you are and what you are about, and you know of the healing that has taken place in Mary's life through you. You know that her heart is pure, much more so than those who sit in judgment of her.

You look up and turn your focus to Simon, your host. Embarrassed that he is staring at you, he diverts his eyes. You call his name and ask him a question. He looks at you.

Are you uncomfortable in the presence of deep, pure love?

Day 5
Luke 7:36-47

Draw an imaginary picture of the dining room in which this dramatic moment occurs. Place yourself in Jesus' position; imagine his thoughts and feelings as he receives Mary's gift.

The aroma of the perfume pervades the room. You know that you will be questioned by the disciples about this moment, and you want everyone to catch the significance of what you are doing and saying.

Imagine the electricity in the air when you look straight into the eyes of Simon. Guided always by your heavenly father, you know what is in this man. You speak directly and pointedly to him. He may be your host, but you hold the power, a power given to you by your heavenly father.

Hear your voice, bold and confident, as you reveal the truth to Simon and force him to face it. Watch his face as you make your case, laying out the difference between the way he has treated you and the way Mary has. See a flicker of recognition in his eyes.

Glance around the room and search the faces of the disciples and Simon's friends. You want everyone there to get the point. This is a significant moment.

Turn your attention to Mary, kneeling at your feet. Let the room grow quiet. Allow the truth to echo in the stillness.

If caught in political intrigue, where would you get your guidance?

Day 6
Luke 7:36-49

Visualize yourself as Jesus, confronting Simon and his hypocrisy. Put yourself in Jesus' place, teaching the disciples important truth.

Feel the compassion of Jesus when he lets himself be anointed by Mary, the harlot, in the presence of other people. Feel the tenderness in his demeanor as he allows himself to receive the love of a women whom he has healed. Sense his total and complete command of what, for other men, would be a compromising position.

Hear the silence in the room after the exchange between Jesus and Simon. Notice the stillness of the servants; it is as if everyone is positioned in suspended animation, waiting to see what will happen next. So far, nothing has been ordinary.

As Jesus, you reach out and touch Mary's shoulder. She looks up into your eyes. By all reason she should be afraid because of what she has done, but in your presence there is nothing but pure love.

Hear your words to her, "Your sins are forgiven." Aligned with your heavenly father, you extend to her the mercy and grace that will make her whole. At this moment you know that your heavenly father's healing work through you is now complete. Notice the pain of the past slip away, replaced by the translucent joy of being set free.

How does the Living Christ feel when you accept his forgiveness?

Day 7
Luke 7:36-50

On this day you replay in your imagination the scene in Simon's house. Today focus on the heart of Christ. Feel his compassion and love. Feel the tenderness he has toward Mary. Feel his joy in knowing that she is now transformed, freed from the bonds of sin and shame and ready to walk in a new life.

As Jesus, you are aware of the buzz in the room, a sound with which you have grown well acquainted. You hear the whispers of speculation. You are fully aware of the doubts, cynicism, and skepticism. You don't mind meeting honest doubt; it is the people's resistance to seeing the truth played out that discourages you.

Look around the room into the faces of doubt. Scan the faces of your disciples. See that they are still avoiding the truth you bring and the reality of who you are. Be aware of the ways that fear and pride hold the dinner guests in icy grips. Feel your heart ache with longing for them to accept the way your heavenly father wants for them.

You turn to Mary. Focus on where the energy is; place your attention in the place where there is an open mind and an open heart. This is where you want to do your work. This is where the Heavenly Father wants you to concentrate your attention. Your voice is quiet and tender as you bless this woman.

In this drama, would you play the part of Mary, Simon, or Jesus?

254

SURRENDER
Jesus in Gethsemane

Matthew 26:36-46

Day 1
Matthew 26:36

Envision a rugged path leading up to a garden of olive trees. See the dark, twisted wood of the trees, shadowy and sinister in the dusk. Hear the eerie sounds of early evening. The cool air causes you to shiver.

As Jesus, you are making your way to one of your favorite places to pray. This time you feel the heaviness of your heart; it is almost unbearable. You try to breathe, but grief is clutching your lungs and heart.

You have just shared a time of closeness and warmth with your disciples. Now they are walking with you to Gethsemane.

You want to be with them, but you know that you must spend some time alone with your heavenly father. You want to tell them what is ahead, but you know that even now they cannot fully understand. Besides, you need to sort out some things in your own mind.

Become aware of the tension in your shoulders. It is as if you are carrying the weight of the whole world on them. Look down at your feet on the pathway. Everything has led to this moment in time, and you know it. This is one of those "fullness of time" moments, but this is one you don't want.

Imagine what it was like for Jesus to come to the end of his ministry on earth.

Remember a time when something good ended. How did you get through that time?

Day 2
Matthew 26:36-38

Walk with Jesus up the rugged path into the garden of Gethsemane. See the gnarled, familiar trees. Make your way deep into the garden to your familiar resting place.

As Jesus, you tell the disciples to wait for you. You look at each one, knowing that in a short while everything about your relationship with them will be changed. You notice the fatigue in their eyes, so you tell them to sit down. Your own fatigue is almost unbearable.

Beckoning to your inner circle—Peter, James, and John—you move deeper into the garden. You look closely at these three friends and tell them about your anguish. You ask them to stay and pray with you.

You look into their faces and see fear and uncertainty, so you urge them to stop where they are and wait for you.

This is one of those moments that only you can experience. No one else can walk through this struggle. No one else can wrestle with the realities of the moment. Neither of these three men, as strong and vital as they are, can do your inner work for you.

You fall down on your knees on the hard, stony ground. Kneeling before a huge boulder, you weep. In the silence of the night air you experience the aloneness of humanity. Here, in this garden, you wrestle with God all by yourself.

When you have to struggle by yourself, what do you do?

Day 3
Matthew 26:36-39

Imagine yourself as Jesus alone in the garden of Gethsemane. Hear the sounds of the night. Feel the cool air on your body. Put yourself in his position. Feel the agony of his heart.

This is the end of the road, at least for this part of life. This is where you must separate from the friends you have made, the work you love, and the vision you have followed. This is the time to face the unfinished business, uncompleted tasks, and unfulfilled longings.

This is the moment when you acknowledge the reality that the drama of your life has to play itself out according to the script. As painful as it is, you must surrender to the sovereignty of God your father and to the mission that is uniquely yours.

In your humanity you wrestle with God. You bargain with Him. The battle between you is fierce, and yet you know that the ultimate act must be the surrender of your will to your father's. . . . If it just didn't have to hurt so much!

It is in the moment of surrender when you can finally pray, "I'll do it your way," that the tension in you begins to subside. It is in the moment of yielding to the will of the Father that the fierceness of the moment recedes.

In the stillness of the garden you let go of all that has been. You agree to the plan. You let God be God.

What is the process of surrender to God like for you?

Day 4

Matthew 26:36-42

Picture yourself as Jesus, standing up in the dark garden. Feel the tension in your body. Listen to the sounds of the wind blowing through the branches of the olive trees. Take a deep breath and smell the familiar aromas of the outdoor sanctuary where you have spent many hours in prayer. Taste the saltiness of your tears.

Imagine yourself turning around and walking back toward the place where you left your friends. You want to share with them the process of surrender you have just experienced. You must teach them, too, that their obedience must always be to the Father's will. You want them to learn the power in trusting and obeying the will of God.

You walk along the path, ready to talk to them, only to discover that they are fast asleep. You stop, shocked and dismayed. You had asked them to pray with you.

As Jesus, you stand there and experience the absolute darkness of loneliness. These, for whom you are about to give your life, are asleep. These on whom you are counting to carry on the important work that can open blind eyes, release prisoners, and set captives free are asleep.

You stand there, alone. A part of you feels the pain of abandonment; another part has deep compassion for these, your friends. Hear yourself admonish Peter. See yourself turn and walk back into the garden to pray.

What is it like to be alone in your greatest trial?

259

Day 5

Matthew 26:42

As Jesus, walk back into the garden area where you are accustomed to praying. You need and want human companionship in this struggle, but you know that this is a road you must walk by yourself. This is your own path of suffering. You want to make sure that you are following God's will.

You long for someone to sit with you in silence and be with you in this terrible moment. You thought that Peter, James, and John would be there for you, but you see now that they cannot bear to witness your anguish. Your heart breaks, but you understand. Perhaps they don't realize what you are feeling.

See yourself falling down on your knees before a huge stone for an altar. Again you dialogue with your heavenly father. Still you resist the reality of the challenge, and you wrestle with God. Is there, you ask Him over and over, another way to show the full extent of your love and His for humankind? Is there any other way to do what He wants you to do?

Weeping, you come to the place where there are no words adequate for expressing the anguish of your heart, so you wait in the silence. This is the darkest night you have known; this is the dark night of your soul. There are no easy answers. There is no way out, except to yield your will to the will of God. There is no escape from the pain of the problem; there is no exit except in surrender. Once again you say, "I'll do it your way."

What is the one thing you know you must surrender to God?

Day 6

Place yourself in the shoes of Jesus. Stand up as he would and walk away from the stone altar.

Feel the beating of your heart as the intensity of your motion increases. Notice the tightness in your chest as you go once again to your friends.

Stand, looking at them as they sleep. Feel the despair of counting on your friends, only to be abandoned in your darkest hour.

Turn around and walk back into the garden. Find your stone altar again and kneel before it. Feel the pain of your calling and purpose swell up in your heart one more time.

The third time you pray, all resistance ebbs from you. You let go and release your life and purpose into the hands of God. This time all the wrestling stops. You sit in the still, quiet, holy moment when you know that the work of surrender is over. Your fighting and grieving are finished. You wait.

You are spent, exhausted, and weary. Strangely, though, once you let go, a new energy begins to emerge. You feel the peace that passes all understanding. Aligned with the perfect will of God, you are ready to face the next scene in your life.

What in your life is so challenging that you must continue to surrender your will, your life, and that thing to God several times before you get to the peace that passes understanding?

Day 7
Matthew 26:36-46

In the role of Jesus, reenter the scene in the moment of surrender. Sit and experience the release that follows. Experience the moment when you know that you are fully aligned with the will of God.

Now you must do the next thing indicated, so you stand up and get your bearings. You wipe your brow and tears with your sleeve. You swallow hard and breathe deeply. You summon all the strength you have, and then lean into the infinite strength of your heavenly father who never leaves you, not even for a moment. You know that even if it seems He is absent, He is not, and you know that there is nowhere you can go where He is not present.

Turn around. Walk back down the familiar path in the darkness. Look around you and say goodbye to the sacred place where you have been at home with God. Let go of all attachment to this natural sanctuary. Detach from this time and place so that you can be and do all for which you were created. Relinquish the old and walk into the will of God for your life.

Hear yourself wake the disciples. You are filled with sadness for them and grief at leaving them, but you know there is something better awaiting all of you. Hear the gentleness in your voice. Hear the firmness and resolve as you tell them what time it is. It is the fullness of time.

Describe the peace you have experienced when you have finally surrendered your will and your life to the care of God. How does it feel to let go and let God take over?

LOVE'S WAY
The Cross Event

Matthew 26:47-75; 27:27-55
John 19:17-27

Day 1

Matthew 26:47-56

Put yourself in the position of Jesus, talking with the disciples in the garden of Gethsemane. You have just gone through the wrenching act of surrender to the will of God. Your disciples are asleep and unaware of what has happened in you.

Enter this scene as Jesus when Judas walks up the hill. How do you feel as you watch this friend and disciple approach you? Feel the calm, cool composure of God descend upon you.

As you watch Judas draw near, you realize that this composure is God's gift to you, and you open your heart wide to receive it. You recall the terrible struggle of bringing your own will into conformity with the will of your heavenly father. Now He has met you at the point of your need to see you through the results of that surrender.

You hear Judas' greeting. He kisses you, and your heart almost breaks. You call him "friend" and tell him to do his deed quickly. You are aware of the disciples, shocked and still.

Feel the harsh hands of the soldiers on your arms. Feel the roughness of them as they push you around. Hear their curses. Smell the strong wine on their breath. You keep your eyes fixed on Judas, but everything in your heart cries out to your father. These men must be terribly weak to have to take you by such force. They must be terribly scared to have to act so tough.

When you surrender to God, do you assume life will be smooth?

264

Day 2

Matthew 26:47-56

Today enter the scene when the soldiers seize Jesus. Smell the sickening stench of power gone awry. Hear the raucous voices. Watch Judas stand over to the side of the action, a smirk on his face.

See Peter pull his sword and cut off the ear of a soldier. See yourself heal the man, even in this, your hour of need. Hear the quiet firmness of your voice chide Peter and the soldiers.

Feel the blows of the soldiers and the sting of their ropes against your flesh. Experience the discomfort of being shoved and pushed and the indignity of losing your balance.

Worse than the physical pain, however, is what you see out of the corner of your eyes. Can it be? Is it possible? You shudder. A low moan escapes your lips.

It is true. One by one, your friends turn away from you. One runs frantically down the hillside. Another backs away from you, tripping on a stone. Still another slips away quietly, almost sneaking away from the action.

There you are, abandoned by the very ones in whom you had placed your hopes and your heart. These are the ones you had let into your life. These are the men you had loved with an everlasting love.

Alone with your betrayer and the soldiers, you bow your head and weep.

Who has betrayed you? Whom have you betrayed? How did it feel?

Day 3
Matthew 26:57-67

Imagine yourself as Jesus, being dragged through the streets of Jerusalem. Feel the indignity of the whole sordid affair deep in your bones. Feel the shame of being made a spectacle.

Imagine yourself standing before Caiaphas, the high priest. Look unflinching into his eyes. Be fully aware of the crowd that is watching you, looking hard for a crime to pin on you.

Breathe deeply as you call on the power and presence of the Living God to sustain and support you. Call out to your heavenly father, in the recesses of your own heart, and hear Him comfort you.

You hear your voice, speaking words of power and confidence. You are outwardly calm, though your heart and mind are raging with the injustice of the whole event.

Suddenly, under the guidance of your father, you are able to see beneath the masks of every person around you. You see only fear. That fear is scabbed over with pride and arrogance, the drive for power, and the need to be right. But underneath it all lies simple fear.

You gaze into the eyes of your accusers and see empty hearts and closed minds. Silently, you extend your heart of love to each one. Silently, you forgive.

When you are in trouble, are you able to stay centered in the presence of God? Do you stay connected to him?

Day 4
Matthew 26:69-75

With the heart of Jesus, feel the shame of the insults hurled in your direction. Feel the contempt hit your heart as the spit from the mouths of the soldiers hits your flesh. Experience the confusion of chaos raging all around you. Experience, at the same time, the calm composure within.

Even as the soldiers mock and beat you, you become aware of Peter's presence in the courtyard. Your heart reaches out to him. Silently, you call his name and plead with him to come near to you.

You are aware that a young servant girl approaches Peter. Your heart sinks. Who would have thought that Peter would do his deed at the motivation of a little servant girl?

"Don't do it, Peter!" you want to scream, but you dare not. You know that whatever he does will not change the course of events for you, but you do not want him to live with the awful feelings of guilt and shame. How hard it is to see someone you love punished by the choices they make! How difficult it is to know that someone has locked himself up in a prison of his own making!

You hear the rooster crow; your heart sinks. You feel the sting of Peter's denial of your friendship, but how much worse it is to know what he has done to himself.

In what ways do you betray the Living Christ today? When you betray him, are you even aware of what you are doing?

Day 5
Matthew 27:27-44

Imagine yourself as Jesus stripped and scourged. Feel the degradation of being draped with a royal robe and then spit upon. Experience the pain of the crown of thorns. Hear the jeers and insults of the mob. Know that you are being put through this torment and torture by people who don't have a clue what they are doing or why they are doing it.

Look into the eyes of your tormentors. See through to the emptiness in their souls. Move through the raging faces and contemptuous eyes and see the fear. Only fear can make people become so inhumane. Only fear can motivate such hatred.

Imagine yourself as Jesus being pushed and shoved, shamed and humiliated. Hear people shouting your name, often with a curse.

Imagine being derided and ridiculed by the crowds, knowing that you have the power to stop the procedures. Feel the suffering in your physical body, but even more, imagine the degradation of getting through the streets of Jerusalem.

Imagine yourself falling to the ground under the weight of the heavy wooden cross. How does it feel when Simon of Cyrene is forced to carry the cross?

When you go through your most severe tests, how do you keep yourself in the presence of God who is always present with you?

Day 6

John 19:17-27

As Jesus, walk up the craggy slopes of Golgotha. Feel the weakness in your legs. See your feet as they slip beneath you. Hear the harsh voice of a soldier tell you to stand up and walk.

At the top of the hill you look up and see two crosses on either side of your cross, which is now being hammered into the ground. You see the mocking sign, and you wrench. These people don't know what they are doing.

Suddenly you sense a soft presence beside you. You turn and look into the eyes of your mother. With the strength left within you, you weep. Does she know that you have not let her down? Does she realize that this is not the final chapter?

You look deep into her face, and the two of you connect heart to heart. She may not understand the whole picture, but she understands enough.

"Goodbye." You mouth the words to her as the soldiers shove you toward the cross.

You turn and search the crowd. Your heart leaps when you see the women standing there. And there is John.

"Take care of my mother," you tell him. You know that he will. And then you surrender to the inevitable.

What is it like to have someone believe in you, no matter what?

Day 7
Matthew 27:45-55

The cross event is still another line mortals cannot cross in fully experiencing the death of Jesus. We can, however, identify with Jesus in his experience of the absence of God.

Imagine what it is like to hang on a criminal's cross, suspended above people who are throwing dice for your clothing.

Imagine a terrible darkness descending over you as the pain of dying becomes excruciating. The defeat seems unbearable. The process of letting go of what has been good, rich, and wonderful is now almost over. In the darkest hour it seems that God has forsaken you. The physical pain is bad enough, but the feeling that God has left you is unbearable. You scream out, begging God to tell you why He has left you, and the sounds of the silence are deafening.

Suddenly though, wracked by physical pain and emotional anguish, you know that even the ability to cry out to God is evidence of God's presence with you. In the moment of crying out you are met with the silence that is filled with the voice of love. In that deepest darkness you encounter the light of the Living God. In the moment of extreme anguish you know that you and the Father are one and that the one whom you are seeking has never, ever let you out of His sight. You, who have taught others that there is nowhere they can go where God is not, are met in your anguish by His presence.

Cry out to God as you have need. The one whom you seek seeks you. How do you get through the moments when you feel that God has abandoned you?

KNOW MY PRESENCE

*He who loves me will be loved by my Father, and
I too will love him and show myself to him. (John
14:22)*

*And surely, I am with you always, even to the
very end of the age. (Matthew 28:20)*

Emmanuel.
God with us.
Presence.

Through the awesome mystery and power of the Holy Spirit,
the holy, transcendent God draws near to His creation and
His children to comfort and confront, to protect and guide.
God is alive and active within creation, attempting to draw all
people to His heart.

"God is everywhere," a wise man proclaims, "and so you
might as well get acquainted with him." Those who are willing will see the presence and power of God in everyday life.
Those who are willing to listen will hear the amazing sym-
phony of God in all the world. The people who are willing to
step out into the place of not knowing, the place of dynamic
faith, will come to know the constant presence of the one who
draws near.

Where is God in Christ showing up in your life right now?
Could it be through the door of loss or through your greatest
need?

DRAWING NEAR
Jesus' Appearance to Mary

John 20:10-18

Day 1
John 20:10-13

Take a giant leap into your imaginative world and call on all of your creative powers to place yourself in the place of Jesus after the resurrection. Admittedly, no one can move fully into that experience, but by exploring the possibility, everyone can know the heart of Jesus a little bit more. Having even the slightest bit of understanding expands our hearts and transforms us into the image of Christ.

Picture yourself as Jesus, returning to your burial site. In a different form, one that only God understands, you stand at a distance, looking at its sinister opening in the side of the hill. All of the pain of that experience is now behind you, and you look at the burial site as if it belonged to someone else.

You notice Mary, leaning against the doorway of the burial cave. She is weeping, and your heart breaks for her. You know the depth of faith that is in her heart. More important, you know what she has been through to come to the place of faith and trust in you.

You watch her, knowing that her heart and mind are so open to receiving a fresh glimpse of grace. Her faith has prepared her to see, and you want to give her the special gift of your presence. Sorrow has carved a deep well in her that can now be filled with great joy. You want to comfort her. You wait for the perfect moment.

Can you believe that the Living Christ wants to comfort you?

Day 2

John 20:10-14

Again make the leap of faith into the experience of Jesus. Picture the scene outside the burial site of Jesus as if you were the Risen Christ. Now, but in a different form and a different way, you are aware of the night air and the feel of death in this place. You are in the situation, but not of it. You stand there, hidden in the night, but you see everything.

See yourself step out of the shadows and move closer to the tomb. You see the angels, dressed in white, on either side of the opening to the burial cave. You can hear Mary weeping.

You hear the angels ask her why she is weeping, and when she turns to answer them, you want to cry aloud. You wait, though, for the right moment to reveal yourself. There is a necessity for the fullness of time in everything.

You hear her familiar voice, now heavy with grief, explain to the messengers that you had been taken away. Her confusion and heartbreak touch you deeply.

You take a few more steps toward the tomb, and Mary turns to face you. She is curious, but only slightly interested in who you are. After all, she is accustomed to seeing you in only one way. It will take her awhile to learn to recognize you in this form.

You stand there and wait. You realize that you must identify yourself to her. Grief has blinded her to your presence and availability.

Ask the Living Christ to make you able to see where he is. What does he want to say to you today?

Day 3
John 20:10-15

Using your gift of imagination, see the scene in front of the burial site of Jesus. Look overhead at the clear sky. Notice the stars scattered here and there. Hear the night song of a bird, the sound of a cricket, and the soft, gentle weeping of Mary.

As you re-create this scene, imagine what is in the heart of Jesus. Ponder the great restraint he shows as he waits for the right moment to reveal himself to Mary. Consider the ways the Living Christ waits even now for the right moment to reveal himself to you.

As Jesus, hear your voice as you ask Mary a question. You are gentle and quiet; you don't want to startle her. After all, seeing you here could be unnerving.

You wonder if you expected her to recognize you immediately. Surely she would if only she would quit looking at the tomb and focus on you. She hasn't yet learned that you are not among the dead and that to keep on looking there is futile.

She glances at you and then looks away. She is more concerned about finding your body than anything else. Little does she know that there is something far greater for her on the other side of her grieving.

You step closer to her, near enough to see her furrowed brow. You sense her anguish and know that once she can recognize that you are with her, all will be well.

Are you looking for the Living Christ in the wrong places?
Is he right in front of you? Are you blinded by the past?

Day 4

John 20:10-16

Imagine yourself as Jesus outside his burial site. Look it over. See the rough cave, the small entrance, and the two angels on either side of the door. Hear the gentle rushing of wind in the trees. Feel the cool night air. Watch Mary and feel her grief.

Feel the expectancy of greeting Mary, your friend and disciple. With the eyes of compassion, see this one whose inner life was once dominated by the demons of fear and guilt, shame and anger. Remember her faithfulness to you. She will be a worthy carrier of the good news of your resurrection. It is Mary who will spread the word that you could not be confined to the tomb.

Step still closer to her. Hear your voice as you call her name.

"Mary," you say, and then you wait.

Will it be enough to say her name? Will your voice speaking her name penetrate through the layers of grief?

You wait, and in the waiting you recall the names of all your friends, the disciples who followed you and learned from you. You want to call each by name. How much you yearn for each one to recognize you, to see you for who you are and for who you want to be with them.

You take another step toward Mary and then wait.

Could it be that the Living Christ is speaking your name, calling to you to see him with you today? Where in your world is he?

Day 5
John 20:10-16

Recall a time when you came upon a friend when you had not seen in a long time. Experience the feeling of anxiety as you wonder if the person will recognize you. You wonder if you have aged so much that the person will not know you. Maybe you have changed so much in one way or another that you will have to identify yourself.

Recall the moment of pleasure when there is a spark of recognition, the years fall away, and you are once again connected. Feel the joy of being recognized for who you are.

Recall a time when you have been willing to lay down the roles you have played and the masks you have worn and let yourself be seen for who you are. Remember the relief and freedom at being accepted and loved for who you are, as you are.

Re-create in your mind's eye the scene in front of the burial site of Jesus. Recall all the sensations of sight and sound.

Stand as Jesus in the moment of exhilaration when Mary sees you, knows you, and calls you by name. Watch as her sorrow turns to joy and her grief to gladness. Watch as Mary's whole body is energized and her voice takes on the lilt of celebration.

What is going through your mind in that moment, knowing that Mary does not yet have a full grasp of your new form and does not know the ways of this new relationship you would have with all of your disciples.

Imagine the joy of the Living Christ when you finally see him. What is it like for him when you recognize his presence with you?

Day 6
John 20:10-17

Reenter this dynamic moment in the life of the resurrected Christ at the moment when Mary recognizes him and calls him by name. As Jesus, hear her call you "Teacher" and experience the joy of being recognized.

Picture yourself as Mary moves toward you, arms outstretched to welcome and embrace you. See the relief and exhilaration on her face Remember all the times she has turned to you for counsel and guidance. Remember the transformation that has taken place in her whole life and the deep gratitude she has always shown you.

Imagine the moment when you must set the boundaries of this new order. Quickly you must redefine your relationship with her, just as you will with all the other disciples and followers.

You speak authoritatively, and she stops. She realizes that things are different, but she is not afraid. Neither is she put off by your reserve with her. Mary's open mind and heart make her such a good disciple.

You set the boundaries. You explain briefly how things are, and then you tell her what to do.

As Jesus, you watch her face and know that her childlike faith is the faith of one whose life has been radically altered. How pliable she is! How eager she is to obey!

Are you pliable enough to sense the instruction of the Living Christ? Will you obey him even if you don't understand?

Day 7
John 20:10-18

Relive the account of Jesus' appearance to Mary, moving from the darkness and heaviness of the first moments of the scene to the light and energy of the last. Feel the tone and mood of the encounter between Mary and Jesus shift as she moves from blindness to sight, from grief to gladness.

Placing yourself in Jesus' position, experience the incredible joy of Mary's instantaneous obedience to your instruction. If only all people could follow your guidance so quickly and eagerly. If only everyone had the openness and willingness to trust you as she does.

You watch her turn and run down the pathway, and you smile to yourself. What a great thing you have done for her, commissioning her to be the first one to tell the Good News to the disciples.

You can see her now, rushing into the room where the disciples are huddled in fear and grief. There she will be, a woman once scorned and tormented, shouting the Good News, "I have seen the Lord!"

You move to your next assignment, basking in the pleasure of knowing that what you have done for Mary when you healed her was one thing, but what you have done for her tonight—giving her the privilege of being the announcer of your resurrection to a group of men—is quite another.

There you are, Jesus, still turning things upside down!

From what unexpected source have you heard the Good News?

MAKING ALL THINGS NEW
Jesus on the Emmaus Road

Matthew 28:19-20
Luke 24:13-49

Day 1
Luke 24:13-16

After the resurrection, Jesus, guided always by the Heavenly Father, appeared to people in order to finish the work he had started and to put in place the continuation of that work. The compassionate heart of the Son of Man always led him to meet the immediate needs of his followers.

In this scene put yourself in his place and get in touch with the deep love he has for his friends and followers. Imagine how it is to join two of your followers as they make their way back home to Emmaus following the terrible events of the crucifixion in Jerusalem. As you watch them, you notice the dejection and disappointment. You hear the confusion in their voices, and your heart goes out to them.

These are men who had taken a big risk to follow you. They had counted on you to do great and wondrous things, and then they had to face the reality of your death on a criminal's cross.

These are men who had challenged the old ways, perhaps having to answer to family and friends about why they were willing to take up with you, an itinerant teacher.

How will you meet their present need? What can you do to lift the heaviness in their hearts?

Is there something in your life right now that is a disappointment to you? Imagine Jesus drawing near to you.

Day 2
Luke 24:13-24

Spend some time in silence before you imagine yourself in this scene. Take time to center yourself in the presence of God. Commit this time of meditation and imaginative praying to Him. Ask the Holy Spirit to draw near to you just as the Risen Christ drew near to his followers on the road to Emmaus.

As Jesus, see the path beneath your feet. Hear the voices of the two men, talking with each other. Feel your heart go out to them as you hear them trying to make sense of what does not make sense. Feel your own compassion as they try to comfort and console each other.

When the moment is right, you make yourself visible to them and ask them a question. Hear the disbelief in the voice of Cleopas. How could you not know what had happened in Jerusalem?

You ask them to explain, so they tell you the story of your life from their perspective.

You listen carefully to their account, knowing that they see from such a limited perspective. It is not their fault that they cannot see the whole picture; they are blinded by their grief and humanity.

You wait for the right moment to give them a broader perspective and help them see the events in Jerusalem from the viewpoint of your father. You can hardly wait to see the light dawn in their faces when they recognize you.

If the Living Christ were to ask you to articulate to him the exact nature of your burden right now, what would you say?

Day 3
Luke 24:13-29

Paint the visual image of three men walking along a dusty road, talking with each other. See the clear blue sky and sunlight on their faces. Hear the song of a bird and the wind rustling through the trees.

Imagine yourself as Jesus, knowing that you can enter only so far into the experience of the Risen Christ and that you must stop at the place where his holiness begins. Nevertheless, imagine how it would have been for him to have been talking to two of his followers who did not yet recognize him.

You have listened to them give their account of your crucifixion in Jerusalem. You know their limited and limiting view of what happened to you.

Hear your voice break in and tell them how foolish they are. Starting with Moses, you set your whole life and your lifework in the context of Jewish history. The men listen with rapt attention, but still they do not recognize you. You wait until the perfect moment to make yourself known to them.

See yourself as the three of you approach the village. You watch for cues from them. See them stop in front of a home. You appear to be walking on. They invite you to stay with them, and you do just that. Picture yourself going through the door of this house.

If the Living Christ articulated his perspective of one of your burdens right now, what would he say? Would you listen to him?

Day 4

Luke 24:13-35

As Jesus, walk into the house in this scene. See one of the men greet his family and introduce you to them. Notice everything about the room where you are standing. Feel the welcome of the host. Listen to the guidance of your heavenly father in the still, small voice that never leaves you.

Imagine yourself as Jesus, sitting down at a low table with your host and his friend. Inhale deeply and savor the aromas of the evening meal. Look around the table and prepare yourself to be the one who opens blind eyes and heals broken hearts in this very room.

Suddenly you reach for the bread that is placed on a simple plate in the center of the table. Feel it, as you hold it with both hands.

You are aware that the host is startled. After all, isn't it he who is supposed to serve you? Inwardly, you smile to yourself.

Hear your voice as you give thanks for the bread. Experience the sensation in your hands as you break the loaf. First you offer a portion of the bread to the host and then to his guests.

You raise the bread to your own lips, signaling that it is time to eat, and in that moment they recognize you.

What a joy it is to be seen for who you are!

Christ is with you right now. Can you see him? Does the awareness of his presence make your heart burn with joy?

Day 5
Luke 24:36-44

Imagine the satisfaction Jesus had when he made a connection with one of his followers. Even in his risen state the responsive Lord must surely have felt joy at being known for who he was. Indeed, he must have delighted in knowing that he had lifted the burden of despair from the hearts of those whom he encountered in the days after the resurrection.

Picture him seeking out the disciples who have gathered together. Imagine him as he observes them talking to each other, trying to integrate the news that he is risen. Does he want to smile to himself now and then as they puzzle over what it all means for them and to them?

Picture yourself as Jesus, standing on the outside of the group of disciples. You search their faces and hearts, and then you speak to them.

"Peace be with you," you say, firmly and gently. You know that in your presence is peace. They will discover this later.

You notice their frightened faces when, at first, they don't realize it is you. So you draw near to them and reveal your heart and wounds to them. You make yourself available and vulnerable for these whom you have loved. You open your own heart and mind, making yourself known to whom you will.

Notice that the recognition happens slowly for some, so you wait, respecting their need to process all that has happened.

What has the Living Christ been trying to help you see?

Day 6
Luke 24:36-49

Picture yourself as Jesus, standing in a room filled with your followers. You look around the room and see the faces that recognize you. You notice the ones who do not, and your heart goes out to them. You know that people come to faith at their own pace, but you long for everyone to see and know you.

Hear your voice as you ask for food. See the rush of a few to make you a plate of broiled fish. See yourself take the plate, sit down, and begin to eat. You savor every morsel. Someone hands you a goblet of wine, and you drink every drop.

You look around the room at your dearest friends and begin to teach them one last time in this form.

What you say must be brief and to the point. In this hour, the hour of saying goodbye, you say the most important things, the things you never want them to forget as they venture out into the unknown without your physical presence. You choose your words carefully and economically.

Look around the room. Find the willing spirits that will not waver. Notice the faces that indicate an open mind and an open heart to be led by the Holy Spirit, the one who is yet to come for them.

As you look at each face, you bless them. You will be with them always, but they will have to learn that. And the way may be perilous.

What do you need to learn from the Living Christ right now?

Day 7

Luke 24:48; Matthew 28:19-20

Imagine yourself as Jesus, sitting with your followers for the last time. Though you are in your risen form, they experience you as the Jesus they have known.

In these last minutes with them, you look deeply into each face and feel your heart filled with love for all of them. You have moved past your grief over leaving them. Now you are entrusting your mission and your work to them.

You have given them the very best of yourself; now it will be up to them to do with you as they will. You have abandoned yourself into their hands. Now you must leave them again.

Hear your voice giving them their task. You state it clearly and succinctly. You hear your voice, forceful and assured. It is a clear directive of what they are to do to cooperate with the Father in bringing about the kingdom of God.

You lead these, your beloved followers, out toward Bethany. Hear the passion in your voice as you bless them one last time.

If only they could know how much you love them. If only they could feel the depth of compassion in your heart for each one. If only they could know that you are with them always.

The Living Christ is with you always and in all places. He never leaves you, not even for a moment. Believe it! Live it! Celebrate the wonder of the risen Christ alive in you. What do you have to lose? What do you have to gain?